The Birth of Reason & Other Essays

by George Santayana

The Birth of Reason & Other Essays

by George Santayana

Edited by Daniel Cory

New York: Columbia University Press

ISBN 0–231–03169–6
ISBN 0–231–10277–1 (pbk.)

Copyright © 1968 Columbia University Press
Library of Congress Catalog Card Number: 68-28397
Printed in the United States of America

c 10 9 8 7 6 5 4 3 2
p 10 9 8 7 6 5 4 3 2 1

CONTENTS

PREFACE

IN GATHERING the essays for this book, I have endeavored
not to saddle Santayana with anything that might be deemed
unworthy of the high level of expository prose he always
maintained in many volumes published during a long life of
continual writing. After all, I was not ransacking an archive
in a desperate quest for bits and pieces that might lead to a
belated Ph.D. degree: it was largely a question of exercising a
"discretion" that he mentioned in his will as desirable in a literary executor. The fact that some of these essays are rather
short—extended "notes" rather than full-blown papers—did
not deter me: to be long-winded is not an unfailing symptom
of insight. I wanted to make sure that an idea had flowered
cleanly on a holograph, albeit in a few trenchant paragraphs.
So there is nothing in this collection of an abortive nature—nothing that should be consigned to the basket by the
desk. I confess that in one or two instances I wished that Santayana had gone over his manuscript again. I felt this espe-

cially in regard to "Friendship." Towards the end of this essay he seems to have embarked on various themes that are perhaps ancillary to the main topic; but I feel that if he had had a "second go" he might have marshaled his points somewhat differently. As it stands, however, the essay is so shot full of light that it had to be included.

It has not always been possible to assign a specific date to the composition of an essay: when I am certain of the year, I have indicated it in the table of contents after the title. The early essays that I have grouped in Part I were all written sometime between 1912 and 1920, while the later essays of Part II were composed roughly between 1935 and 1950. I have been guided not only by an acquired sensitivity to his literary style at different periods of his career, but also by such external indications as the type of paper or color of ink, etc. As for the more philosophical essays that compose Part III, with the exception of "What Is the Ego?" they all belong to a later period. But in the case of an outstanding *homme des lettres,* any distinction between "philosophical" and "literary" in a given body of his work is often dubious, and I have made it here chiefly for the convenience of the reader. For instance, the essay entitled "The Soul at Play" is rather lighthearted—almost jocular in tone, but it does embody a subtle exposition of Santayana's theory of knowledge.

This prompts me to indulge in a more general observation. Since the last world war there has been a sustained "movement" (especially in England) to confine the proper activity of philosophy to an examination of language in use—"linguistic behavorism," or call it what you will. But not so long ago it was still respectable to hold that a philosopher was simply a "lover of wisdom," and there was at least an etymological justification for so considering the vocation of certain individuals. And whether a man happened to be a professor or not was beside the point. If a philosopher could write beautifully and had broad interests, like Schopenhauer or Bradley or Santayana, so much the better. The generous sun of those happy years no longer gilds the towers, nor warms the lawns, of some ancient seats of learning. But I remind myself that there are fashions in philosophy as well as in the desirable length for a lady's skirt, and twenty-five years is a fragment of time when compared with the perennial interest and importance of the great issues of the mind. If Oxford and Cambridge think that they, and they alone, are "doing philosophy" today, we must wait patiently for the pother to peter out in an insular tanglewood of verbal foliage.

In the evening of life in Rome, Santayana was too busy with *Dominations and Powers* to be agitated by a faraway "revolution in philosophy." But did he overlook anything of lasting importance? There is something ridiculous about the career of English philosophy this century: after wrangling for years over the precise status of "sense-data," it has now turned as a last resort to an exclusive consideration of "sentences." What has happened to the imaginative courage, the vision that we normally expect to find in a philosopher *digne de son nom?* Human consciousness may be only an intermittent light that here and there, now and then, grants us a glimpse of an enormous, primordial, and largely indifferent universe.

But this is hardly a good reason for abusing the light we possess. The natural setting of a philosopher is somewhat wider than a common room, and the young "lover of wisdom" ought to be encouraged to do something more than untangle the inevitable knots of his native dialect, or point out triumphantly a few fatuous things that older worthies have uttered in the past. Even granting with Wittgenstein that language is best conceived as a *lebensform,* it is nevertheless just possible that a philosopher could exist without talking, although he might find it difficult to continue talking if he were not alive. In other words, from a cosmic standpoint, all the data of our senses, and all the sentences we utter, are rather superficial complications of a limited number of high-grade organisms. For however we may describe an "external world," there will doubtless be stubborn systems of events (or "things") in a vast causal network that may or may not involve human experience; but for the time being at least there are fellow minds to share consciously our common destiny, no matter how trivial or swollen they may become. If we acknowledged more frankly to ourselves the place of the mind in a rather precarious environment, a sense of natural piety might inform our provincial hours and make them more *philosophical.*

If the innocent reader has been somewhat embarrassed by these sober observations, let me assure him at once that there are lighter essays in this volume that reveal a candid mind on vacation. I am thinking of pieces like "The Philosophy of Travel," "Towers," or "Tom Sawyer and Don Quixote." And if philosophy, as Wittgenstein has suggested, only "begins

when words go on holiday," then everything I have gathered
here is a play of sunshine and shadow. It is the cathartic
effect of all great writers to transform the tragic and comic
sides of the peculiar human predicament into an imagina-
tively acceptable whole—or work of art. But are we wandering from the truth when we exploit the possibilities of language, and in so doing employ the proper "furniture of the
mind"? In normal intercourse words are suffused and carried
by private images and unique feelings. Perhaps "linguistic be-
haviorism" is only a professional obsession of certain myopic
"philosophers" who have either lost the way—or never received the calling. In the embracing movement and seduction
of Santayana's work we can "drown" for a season our petty
preoccupations and admire a zealous champion and defender
of the human imagination. And to deny that such a man is a
philosopher is to betray a rather mean and narrow estimation
of our vocation.

I have been able to include and head the table of contents
with a hitherto unpublished sonnet by Santayana to a Harvard friend. I think it is one of his better sonnets, a fine speci-
men of an early vintage.

DANIEL CORY

Rome, 1967

INTRODUCTION

Herman J. Saatkamp, Jr.

DANIEL CORY, Santayana's close associate and literary secretary from 1927 to 1952, first published *The Birth of Reason* essays in 1968, five years following the hundredth anniversary of Santayana's birth. The essays make noteworthy contributions to Santayana's thought, reaffirming positions he previously developed and advancing his line of inquiry and discussion in many areas. Santayana's insights into history, politics, religion, science, philosophy, and everyday life are not outdated. Although many of the essays were never refined for publication, they reveal Santayana's remarkable skill with the English language, all the more surprising since English was his second language. His style of writing is appealing to educated readers, who are attracted by his penetrating historical and cultural analyses, quick turn of phrase, perceptive account of complex issues, and sage advice. Santayana's philosophical and cultural concerns are ahead of their time. He does not employ the methods of many contemporary philosophers, particularly those with a strong bent toward logic or linguistics. Instead, his discussions converge on current issues concerning foundationalism, belief claims, scientific and religious knowledge, and aesthetics. Recognizing Santayana's achievements, Arthur Danto in 1963 called for a revival of Santayana studies, noting that many philosophers are recapitulating "the intellectual crisis which Santayana helped overcome," breaking through "to a view of things not dissimilar to the one he [Santayana] achieved."[1] In 1985 Hilary Putnam echoed Danto's remarks: "If there has been less attention paid to Santayana's philosophy than to that of Royce or Peirce, this is in large part because his philosophical mood and philosophical intuitions were actually ahead of his time. In many ways he anticipated some of the dominant trends of American philosophy of the present day."[2]

The reissue of the essays of *The Birth of Reason* is a step in the revitalization of Santayana studies that recently has witnessed an increase in publications on Santayana's life and philosophy, the formation of an international society dedicated to the study of Santayana's works,[3] and the funding of a critical edition of his complete literary and philosophical corpus.[4]

Santayana's Life

Dramatic episodes and reflective insights silhouette Santayana's life and philosophy. Migration, separation from parents, life in an alien culture, academic partisan heat, and two world wars are prominent contours of his philosophical and literary achievements. In them Santayana's presence is that of a savant: wise to hidden events, honest in his views of others and of himself, and able to craft an artful, admirable life encircled by unyielding public and private constraints. His philosophical foundations are his naturalism and the Socratic ideal of self-knowledge.

As a naturalist, Santayana maintains that all explanations of events ultimately are rooted in the physical world, but what populates the conscious world of human beings is not reducible merely to the physical. Human values, ideals, and ideas are not material, nor are they subject to scientific investigation. They are the aesthetic qualities of human existence that make life worthwhile, festive, and dramatic. The principal challenge of human life is to know and accept one's natural heritage and environment while crafting a life of value. This is an invitation, not to any supernatural task or world, but to the art of living in everyday human life. The quotidian activities of ordinary existence generate value, beauty, and the good. The perspectives of acceptance and celebration are reflected in his life and writings, and they distinctively mark Santayana as a major literary and philosophical figure of the twentieth century.

In the opening essay of this volume, "The Philosophy of Travel," Santayana says, "The most radical form of travel, and the most tragic, is migration" (10). This comment is revealing since migration characterizes much of Santayana's life, leading one biographer to label him the "vagabond scholar."[5] His fellow countryman, Pablo Picasso, considered the vagabond performing artist as the poetic embodiment of alienated creative genius and spiritual grace.[6] Such characteristics are apt for Santayana's migratory spirit, but he found migration not merely alienating; it was heroic and stimulating: "[I]n travel, as in being born, interest may drown the discomfort of finding oneself in a foreign medium: the solitude and liberty of the wide world may prove more stimulating than chilling. Yet migration like birth is heroic: the soul is signing away her safety for a blank cheque" (10–11).

Santayana's heroic blank check began in Madrid, Spain, where he was born in 1863. His childhood was fated by the Spanish diplomatic backgrounds of his parents and by the distant relations between them. He was the only child of his father but the sixth of his mother, who previously had been married to an American businessman. Both parents were world travelers, familiar with cultural and political differences and with the accidental features that cause human life to flourish and diminish. His father, Agustín Santayana, was well educated, trained as an artist, and served the Spanish government as a diplomat until his early retirement due to ill health resulting from his service in the Philippines.[7] His mother's father was also a Spanish diplomat who, due to the ironic contingencies of politics, once served as the American ambassador to Spain. He died as the Spanish governor of a small Philippine island, leaving his daughter, Josefina, on her own. To provide for herself, she established a successful export business. In time, the new Spanish governor, Agustín Santayana, arrived. For uncertain reasons, Josefina moved to

Manila, met the Bostonian businessman George Sturgis, and married. There were five Sturgis children, three of whom survived infancy. She was left on her own in the Philippines again when her first husband died, but this time she moved to Boston, largely supported by a gift from her husband's brother. The support was necessary since George Sturgis's business ventures had had limited success. Years later, on a chance holiday in Spain, Josefina and Agustín were reunited. They married, and Jorge Agustín Nicolás Santayana was born in 1863. Susan Sturgis, Santayana's half sister, insisted on the name "Jorge" and that he be called "George" after *her* father.[8]

Josefina left Spain when George Santayana was nearly seven, upholding a promise to her first husband to educate the Sturgis children in Boston. Realizing that his son's opportunities were better in America, Agustín moved to Boston with George two years later (1872), but Agustín never adapted to the puritanical, New England culture nor to the Boston climate. After several months he returned to Avila where he maintained a lifelong correspondence with his son,[9] whom he would see again in 1884, when Santayana was a Harvard undergraduate, and then yearly until Agustín's death in 1893.

Santayana's life has three phases: his early years in Spain, forty years in the United States, and forty years of retirement in Europe and England. Gifted and intelligent, he found his student years at Harvard filled with frolic, poetry, and philosophy. He was torn between his allegiances to America and to Spain and Europe. As a professor, increasingly he came to view the American culture as youthful and energetic but shrouded by an anti-intellectual appetite for the production of goods without concern for the quality of life. Harvard, the foremost American academic center, was seen as "taken in" by the promise of progress based on economic gains when, according to Santayana, one needed a central focus on the knowledge and understanding requisite for living well. He found being a professor was too consumed with administrative concerns and academic quibbles, making it difficult to be a full-time writer and scholar. Although his professorship began in 1889, this sense of the nonscholarly and limited nature of the professorate induced him in the mid-1890s to begin planning an early retirement from Harvard. In a letter to a friend in 1892, Santayana expressed the hope that his academic life would be "resolutely unconventional" and noted that he could only be a professor *per accidens,* saying that "I would rather beg than be one essentially."[10] Santayana's unique position at Harvard is highlighted in two of his poetic social criticisms of the American role in the Spanish-American War ("Uncle Sammy's First Wild Oats" and "Spain in America").

In 1893 Santayana underwent a change of heart, a *metanoia,* as he called it. Gradually he altered his mode of living to one more conducive to writing and scholarship. His circle of friends was closer but not as broad, and the regular habits of writing and travel that characterize his later life had their beginnings in these Harvard years.

Three events preceded his *metanoia:* the unexpected death of a young student, witnessing his father's death, and the marriage of his half sister Susana. Santayana's reflections on these events led to an acceptance of the tragic predicament of life and its imaginative release:

Cultivate imagination, love it, give it endless forms, but do not let it deceive you. Enjoy the world, travel over it, and learn its ways, but do not let it hold you ... To possess things and persons in idea is the only pure good to be got out of them; to possess them physically or legally is a burden and a snare.[11]

For Santayana, this conclusion was liberating; it was the ancient wisdom that acceptance of the tragic leads to a lyrical release. His naturalism with its lyrical cry of human imagination sets him apart from his colleagues in the Harvard philosophy department. It is rooted in Aristotle and Spinoza and has its contemporary influences in James's pragmatism and Royce's idealism. But Santayana's focus on and celebration of creative imagination in all human endeavors is one of his distinctive contributions to American thought. This focus, along with his Spanish heritage, Catholic upbringing, and European suspicion of American industry, set him apart in the Harvard Yard.

Several scholars conclude that Santayana was also distinctively homosexual, another characteristic that would set him apart from the standard lifestyles of the Harvard community. The evidence for this is mixed and is drawn largely from allusions in Santayana's early poetry[12] and supported by the known homosexual and bisexual orientation of several of Santayana's friends and associates.

Santayana never married, and he provides no clear indication of his sexual preferences. Attraction both to women and to men seems evident in his early correspondence. The one documented comment about his homosexuality occurred when he was sixty-five. Following a discussion of A. E. Housman's poetry and homosexuality, Santayana remarked, "I think I must have been that way in my Harvard days although I was unconscious of it at the time."[13] Whether homosexual or not, it is clear that Santayana's closest associates were male, not an unusual feature of the all-male university community. If he were a practicing homosexual from his student days on, his life is even more distinctive than previously has been recognized. And if he was a latent homosexual throughout his life, then the cultural and social constraints of public life clearly shape his friendships and career.

Although never officially an American (he retained his Spanish citizenship throughout his life), he is associated with the development of Classical American philosophy along with Peirce, James, Royce, and Dewey. He was widely recognized as a philosopher, poet, critic of culture and literature, and dramatist, making him one of the major *literati* of the time. When he formally announced his retirement in 1911, he had an established international reputation. His first philosophical book, *The Sense of Beauty* (1896), remains to this day an important volume for aesthetics. *Interpretations of Poetry and Religion* (1900) was followed by the five books of *The Life of Reason* (1905–1906), which established Santayana as a major philosophical figure.

Although Santayana's pending retirement had been

known for some time, Harvard's President Lowell asked him to reconsider and, recognizing Santayana's penchant for Europe, made arrangements to rotate his teaching between the Sorbonne and Harvard. Santayana agreed temporarily to this arrangement, but in 1912, after setting in order family matters, he left Harvard and America never to return. His mother, who apparently had been suffering from Alzheimer's disease, died shortly after he left the United States, leaving him an inheritance, which furthered his chances of travel and retirement without significant financial concerns.[14] All financial arrangements he turned over to his half brother, requesting only that he be provided enough to support a modest life, and he pledged that his Sturgis relations would inherit the bulk of his estate. Santayana arranged for his friend Bertrand Russell to take his place at Harvard for the first year. Apparently Harvard hoped to replace Santayana with Russell, but the Harvard atmosphere was equally unappealing to "Bertie."

Free from academia, financial concerns, and American entanglements, he spent the remainder of his life, some of his most productive years, in London, Cambridge, Paris, the Riviera, Madrid, Avila, Florence, Cortina d'Ampezzo, and Rome.

Offers of distinguished chairs followed him throughout his retirement, but he remained steadfast in his commitment to full-time writing rather than the businesslike professorate. He wrote philosophical works such as *Scepticism and Animal Faith* (1923), *Platonism and the Spiritual Life* (1927), and the four books of *The Realms of Being* (1927, 1930, 1938, 1940), but he became widely known for his cultural and literary criticisms in *Winds of Doctrine* (1913), *Egotism in German Philosophy* (1915), *Soliloquies in England* (1922), *Dialogues in Limbo* (1926), and *The Idea of Christ in the Gospels* (1946). Two of his works brought international fame. His novel, *The Last Puritan* (1936), and his autobiography, *Persons and Places* (1944), were best-selling books in the United States as selections of the Book-of-the-Month Club, and he is one of the few philosophers to appear on the cover of *Time* (February 3, 1936).

Although elderly and not in good health, Santayana attempted to leave Rome for Switzerland before World War II. After a long journey he was stopped at the border and turned back because of insufficient papers. His was a complicated case: a Spanish citizen residing in Rome with most of his financial ties in the United States and England. On October 14, 1941, he entered the Clinica della Piccola Compagna di Maria, a hospital clinic run by a Catholic order of nuns, where he lived until his death on September 26, 1952. Since he was not Catholic and did not convert, in spite of some efforts by the nuns and others at the clinic, Santayana asked not to be buried in the consecrated ground of the Roman cemetery. Daniel Cory discovered that the unconsecrated ground was reserved for criminals and the poor. The Spanish government had the final say, dedicating to Santayana its "Panteon de la Obra Pia espanola" in Rome's Campo Verano Cemetery and burying him there with a special stone and a large inscription drawn from *The Idea of Christ in the Gospels.* Cory read lines from Santayana's "The Poets Testament," a poem affirming his naturalistic outlook:

I give back to the earth what the earth gave,
All to the furrow, nothing to the grave.
The candles out, the spirit's vigil spent;
Sight may not follow where the vision went.[15]

Fin de Siècle Hispanic-American

The character of Santayana's life and writings sets him apart
and makes the essays in *The Birth of Reason* important as
we turn to a new century and a new millennium. Histori-
cally the *fin de siècle* calls to question the foundations of
society, science, art, and culture. Santayana, as a turn-of-
the-century figure, carefully examines the basic structures of
society and of individual life. Some of the themes of his
essays reflect his view that the American society and culture
is undergoing significant changes. His only novel, *The Last
Puritan,* gives a literary character to the historical changes
occurring during the transition from the nineteenth to the
twentieth century. For Santayana, this was a transition from
a Great Merchant Society to a more democratic and commercial one, a change that made travel and commodities
more widely available than at any previous time. It was the
finale for a particular class and their ethos, the last of the
puritans, and the opening curtain for a new generation ow-
ing less to their predecessors, harboring more hope for their
future, and recognizing a larger world community. His view
of the celebratory European, free to enjoy life, and the obli-
gated American, bound by habit and activity, carries considerable weight as we turn to the twenty-first century. Much
can be learned from Santayana's Hispanic heritage, shaded
by his sense of being an outsider in America. His writings

capture the apprehension and concern that is apparent as contemporary Americans find their *milieux* fragmented and the historic role of their economic enterprise and government in question.

Santayana's philosophical outlook and publications are not dated by either century, nor do they reflect parochial American or European views. He sees classical philosophical questions arising in each century and in each country. He warns against the age-old demons of ideology and public opinion, counsels for a clear understanding of our biological and social histories, and maintains with Socrates that self-knowledge is the birth of reason.

Public opinion is like the wind; it becomes at times a formidable force, something a man finds himself borne along by or fighting against; yet in itself it is invisible, rises suddenly in gusts and squalls, and mysteriously disappears (101); ... the ideas and the shouts of the public play a thin and inconstant treble (107).

Events flow from causes extraordinarily complex, geographical, biological, psychic and economic; whereas political ideologies represent irresponsible prophecies, or social rivalries and resentments, blind to everything but themselves (162–63).

With festive Spanish irony he refuses to yield to fashion and the march of progress. He wrestles with philosophical and literary questions through classical terms and phrases, providing his own elegance of style and withdrawing from absolute standards imposed on him or by him.

Santayana is known as a genius for epigrams, and some of his witty assertions are a part of our cultural expressions regularly finding their way into news broadcasts, political speeches, and even fund-raising campaigns and cartoons. Among the most famous is his remark about those who cannot remember history. Within the essays of this book there are many others less widely known but worthy of consideration:

The Bible is a wonderful source of inspiration for those who do not understand it (98);

Certainly official minds are not fountains of originality (113);

Fortunately on earth nothing lasts for ever (115);

... philosophers, like fish, move often in schools, and each sect is bitterly exclusive (129);

Kindness, as the name implies, has its root in the family (87);

Friendship belongs to life in the open (79);

... true classicism is the understanding that life is an art within natural limits (27);

There would be less faction and ill-will in the world if people could distinguish their preferences from their information (159);

or, Disinterested insight is permitted to any fish in any river, provided he can get his nose out of the water (110).

Santayana's political outlook is decidedly conservative, although he flirted with a variety of socialisms, particularly those with a materialistic bent. In brief, he believed that freedom is the result of order (natural order), not order the result of freedom: "Freedom is the result of perfect organization. The problem is so to organize ourselves as to become free" (85). This conservatism, Spanish heritage, and his forced residence in Rome during World War II mistakenly led some to consider him a Fascist with sympathies aligned with Mussolini and Hitler. It is now clear that he distinguished himself from these political figures and from the form of National Socialism that evolved in Germany and Italy, although he initially found the new organization and productivity of Italy under Mussolini promising, as he did the socialistic developments in Russia. In 1934 the editor of *The Saturday Review of Literature,* Henry Seidel Canby, asked Santayana for an essay on fascism. Daniel Cory explains that Santayana "was not especially interested in a local regimen in Italy, but in the wider political questions that he later treated in his book on *Dominations and Powers*" (108*n*). In the resulting essay, "Alternatives to Liberalism," Santayana notes the surprise of the liberals at the rise of Lenin, Mussolini, and Hitler. But he sees their rise as a natural result of the sway of public opinion and the pressing need for order. However, the end of the essay serves as a prophesy to the short-lived aspirations of political Titans. He notes the importance of not inserting lies "in the state catechism" (113). The best government "would think on the human scale, loving the beauty of the individual. If their ordinances were sometimes severe under stress of necessity, that severity would be rational, or at least amenable to reason. In such a case, holding truth by the hand, authority might become gentle and even holy" (114–15). But the contemporary scene is different.

Now, on the contrary, we sometimes see the legislator posing as a Titan. Perhaps he has got wind of a proud philosophy that makes the will absolute in a nation or in mankind, recognizing no divine hindrance in circumstances or in the private recesses of the heart. Destiny is expected to march according to plan. No science, virtue, or religion is admitted beyond the prescriptions of the state. Every natural whim is sacred, every national ambition legitimate. Here is certainly an intoxicating adventure; but I am afraid a city so founded, if it could stand, would turn out to be the iron City of Dis. These heroes would have entrenched themselves in hell, in scorn of their own nature; and they would have reason to pine for the liberal chaos from which their Satanic system had saved them. Fortunately on earth nothing lasts for ever; yet a continual revulsion from tyranny to anarchy, and back again, is a disheartening process (115).

Santayana's approach to public discontent and social challenges is both individualistic and naturalistic; for some critics, it is too much of both. Santayana counsels self-knowledge, leading to a cultivation of the art of individualistic living. But Santayana never suggests only one model for human life, and he was careful to avoid suggesting that his life should serve as a model. For him, life was "more speculative, freer, juster, and ... happier,"[16] but "not better" since he accepted no absolute standards. His motto might read: "Each individual to his or her own devices but with the cultivation, wisdom, and habits of the past (the individuals particular past) informing and structuring actions." His guidance is wise. We can learn from his concerns about the deceptions of ideology as when he notes that "Fanaticism consists in redoubling your effort when you have forgotten your aim,"[17] and we can understand his often repeated counsel concerning history: "Those who cannot remember the past are condemned to repeat it."[18]

For organizing and altering political and institutional structures, Santayana's individualistic model may seem inadequate. But for many persons, finding a clear vision of one's own good, pursuing it, and cultivating a life around that perspective, may be the key to surviving and living with dignity in complex and demanding social structures. The alternative, which sounds quite up-to-date, is far less appealing:

But when society is deeply troubled, when men do not know what to do, what to think, what to enjoy, or how to avoid hateful compulsions, then every complaint and every panacea gathers adherents, parties arise, and ideologies fill the atmosphere with their quarrels (107).

Santayana's political aim is to respect all nationalities and governments for their native intelligence and origin, while remaining true to one's heritage without binding one's perspective to any regional outlook. Santayana's boyhood town of Avila, Spain, provides a picturesque model for his native intelligence. Looking through the narrow portals in Avila's memorable wall, a person's horizons open to a larger world even while being secure within the medieval town. Open to the world but true to one's natural self, this was Santayana's guide throughout his life.

This cicerone led him to be a harbinger of important intellectual turns on both sides of the Atlantic: his naturalism, his view of philosophy as literature, his insistence that the nonreligious spiritual life is of major importance in a businesslike and quantitative world, his characterization of the celebration of the good life in a world community, his institutional pragmatism, and his explorations of the practical links binding private and public well being.

The Pursuit of Wisdom: Festive Naturalism

Throughout his long life (1863–1952) Santayana pursued the ancient Greek wisdom of self-knowledge. This pursuit led, for Santayana, to the recognition and acceptance of human action as constrained and contoured by material forces shaping ones own constitution and the environment. Human life is not unique; it is another instance of animal life and is as subject to investigation and scientific explanation as any animal life may be. This naturalistic philosophy is a common sense view of the human animal in a natural environment: humans find themselves in a particular environment with a specific makeup and heritage not of their choosing, and the task of life is to live well within these circumstances. The circumstances determine whether one may live well or not, and, as such, all is fated. But the inchoate determinants of human life may give birth to reason and to spirit. Both these outgrowths of natural circumstances provide dramatic qualities to human existence that liberate it spiritually, not materially, from its tragic predicament.

The birth of reason, generated by the harmony in one's material predicaments, may be followed by the birth of consciousness, or spirit. Spirit is not limited to the undramatic, uncaring, material conditions of one's own being, society, and species. Human consciousness may survey a limitless range of possibilities not existent, not requisite for action, not necessary for survival, but delightful, festive, and eternal. The joint births of reason and spirit make life worthwhile, giving dramatic, festive characteristics to the undramatic and fated world.

The Birth of Reason

In the essay "The Birth of Reason," Santayana writes of the fatal predicament of human life and the mental remove requisite for festive liberation. "[T]he world is my host and myself a guest" (52), but this truth is tragic for human beings. Ongoing, uncaring, material forces host all events, including human actions. This host is "flowing at its own meandering paces through an endless variety of forms" (58). The guest is created and fated by the physical predicament of heritage and environment, but the spirit of human life longs for freedom, for liberation, for life beyond its caged entanglements. This longing generates false beliefs, the most prominent being absolute freedom.

Belief in absolute freedom is self-destructive. It leads to hatred of one's own being and fosters self-deception. The nightmare of absolute freedom stirs with the realization that one's first free choice would limit, load, and poison one's whole future. This first choice, small as it may be, "makes me therefore a created, fated, hypnotized thing compelled to hate my own being" (55).

Abandoning the belief in absolute freedom and accepting ones fated predicament may lead to disinterested pessimism, a pessimism not of gloom but of imaginative and speculative festivity. Santayana writes:

Being in the dumps may enable a man to shake off conventional hypocrisies and to become an impartial sympathizer with all oppressed races and with the inalienable right of every crying child to cry loudly; but only when speculation has lifted a man from the dumps will he become a disinterested pessimist, like my first guides in free thought, Lucretius, Spinoza, and Schopenhauer (49).

Spirit, Santayana's term for consciousness or awareness, arises when the physical elements of the world unknowingly attain harmony. Spirit is "precisely the voice of order in nature, the music, as full of light as of motion, of joy as of peace, that comes with an even partial and momentary perfection in some vital rhythm" (53). Such harmony is temporary, and the disorganized natural forces permit spirit to arise "only spasmodically, to suffer and to fail. For just as the birth of spirit is joyous, because some nascent harmony evokes it, so the rending or smothering of that harmony, if not sudden, imposes useless struggles and suffering" (53). The insecure equilibrium of the natural world must be recognized and accepted before one can celebrate the birth of reason and spirit in the natural world. Such a celebration leads to the delight of imagination and artistry, and to the acceptance of the insecure circumstances of ones liberation. The instability of the physical world makes the celebration all the more significant, makes ones mental remove from fate all the more vital and rich.

The importance of the essays in *The Birth of Reason* is
highlighted by the advanced wisdom of Santayana's reflections. At a few points, his sagacity is distanced and narrowed by his heritage, education, and temperament as in
some of his remarks about Judaism and John Dewey. But
even then, he is open to correction and imaginative play. In
many ways, his perspectives were far ahead of their time,
and they deserve reconsideration and respect. Santayana was
a naturalist before naturalism grew popular; he appreciated
multiple perfections before multiculturalism became an issue; and he naturalized Platonism, updated Aristotle, fought
off idealisms, and provided a striking and sensitive account
of the spiritual life without being a religious believer.

The Birth of Reason & Other Essays

by George Santayana

SONNET TO A HARVARD FRIEND

No flower I bring you but the scentless weed
That in my youth's deserted garden grew
Wherein no zephyr of soft passion blew
Nor gust of anger bent the barren reed.
What advocate have they, to help their need,
These meagre verses, faded, sad, and few
Writ ere I loved you? Not my love of you,
For that proud novice is unused to plead.
Cast them away, and I will others bring
Of richer fragrance, when the summer's prime
Hast burst the late buds of the laggard spring.
And yet, how idle that I then should sing,
Or you should listen, when to judging Time
The heart will speak without the pomp of rhyme.

This sonnet was written by Santayana on the flyleaf of his first book
of poems—*Sonnets and Other Verses* (Stone and Kimball, 1894)—and
given as a graduation present to Guy Murchie on June 20, 1895.

PART I: *Early Essays*

THE PHILOSOPHY OF TRAVEL

HAS ANYONE ever considered the philosophy of travel? It might be worth while. What is life but a form of motion and a journey through a foreign world? Moreover locomotion— the privilege of animals—is perhaps the key to intelligence. The roots of vegetables (which Aristotle says are their mouths) attach them fatally to the ground, and they are condemned like leeches to suck up whatever sustenance may flow to them at the particular spot where they happen to be stuck. Close by, perhaps, there may be a richer soil or a more sheltered and sunnier nook; but they cannot migrate, nor have they even eyes or imagination by which to picture the enviable neighbouring lot of which chance has deprived them. At best their seed is carried by the wind to that better place, or by some insect intent on its own affairs: vegetables migrate only by dying out in one place and taking root in another. For individual plants it is a question of living where

This essay appeared in *Virginia Quarterly Review* (Winter 1964).

they are or not living at all. Even their limbs can hardly move, unless the wind moves them. They turn very slowly towards the light, lengthening and twisting themselves without change of station. Presumably their slumbering souls are sensitive only to organic variations, to the pervasive influence of heat or moisture, to the blind stress of budding and bursting here, or the luxury of blooming and basking and swaying there in the light. They endure in time and expand vaguely in space, without distinguishing or focussing the influences to which they are subject; having no occasion to notice anything beyond their own bodies, but identifying the universe, like the innocent egoists they are, with their own being. If ever they are forced into a new pose, which might be of permanent advantage to them, they revert to the perpendicular when the force is relaxed; or if the pressure has been brutal, they may remain permanently a little bent, as if cowed and humbled by the tyrant into a life-long obliquity. Often all the trees in a row lean to the prevalent leeward, like a file of soldiers petrified on the march, or a row of statues unanimously pointing at nothing; and perhaps their crookedness may prove merciful to them, and enable them more comfortably to weather the storm, in forgetfulness of perfection. If it were not that the young shoots still tend to grow up straight, I would almost believe that distortion had become their proper ideal and was no longer distortion but character. Certainly among mankind, when vices become constitutional, they turn into worldly virtues; they are sanctioned by pride and tradition, and called picturesque, sturdy, and virile. Yet to a wider view, when their forced origin is considered, they still seem ugly and sad. Sin is sin, though it be original, and misfortune is misfortune so long as the pristine soul stirs within the crust of custom, tortured by the morality which is supposed to save it.

The shift from the vegetable to the animal is the most complete of revolutions; it literally turns everything upside down. The upper branches, bending over and touching the ground, become fingers and toes; the roots are pulled up and gathered together into a snout, with its tongue and nostrils protruding outwards in search of food; so that besides the up-and-down and inwards-and-outwards known to the plant, the animal now establishes a forward-and-back—a distinction possible only to travellers; for the creature is now in perpetual motion, following his own nose, which is itself guided and allured by all sorts of scents and premonitions coming from a distance. Meantime the organs of fertility, which were the flowers, sunning themselves wide open and lolling in delicious innocence, are now tucked away obscurely in the hindquarters, to be seen and thought of as little as possible. This disgrace lies heavy upon them, prompting them to sullen discontent and insidious plots and terrible rebellions. Yet their unrest is a new incentive to travel, perhaps the most powerful and persistent of all: it lends a great beauty to strangers, and fills remote places and times with an ineffable charm. Plants had no such possibilities; they could not make a chance acquaintance, they could not fall in love, and I am not sure that in their apparent placidity they were really happier. There is something dull in the beauty of flowers, something sad in their lasciviousness; they do not crave, they do

not pursue, they wait in a prolonged expectation of they
know not what, displaying themselves to order like a child
decked out for a holiday, vaguely proud, vaguely uncomfort-
able, vaguely disappointed. The winds are impatient wooers,
and a shower of gold-dust is a poor embrace. They fade,
thinking they are still virgins; they drop their petals in sad-
ness, and shrink nun-like into a withered stalk; there is an
acrid savour in their elderly sweetness: they believe they have
missed something which they pretend to despise. Yet they are
mistaken; they have altogether fulfilled their function: they
are grandmothers without knowing it. They were married
long ago, with only a faint sense of being present at their own
wedding; they have borne children as is consonant with their
nature, painlessly and in quite other places; they have
marched unawares, veiled and honoured as mothers, in the
procession of time.

In animals the power of locomotion changes all this pale
experience into a life of passion; and it is on passion, although we anaemic philosophers are apt to forget it, that intelligence is grafted. Intelligence is a venture inconceivably
daring and wonderfully successful; it is an attempt, and a
victorious attempt, to be in two places at once. Sensibility to
things at a distance, though it may exist, is useless and unmeaning until there are organs ready to avoid or pursue these
things before they are absorbed into the organism; so that it
is the possibility of travel that lends a meaning to the images
of the eye and the mind, which otherwise would be mere
feelings and a dull state of oneself. By tempting the animal to
move, these images become signs for something ulterior,

something to be seized and enjoyed. They sharpen his attention, and lead him to imagine other aspects which the same thing might afford; so that instead of saying that the possession of hands has given man his superiority, it would go much deeper to say that man, and all other animals, owe their intelligence to their feet. No wonder, then, that a peripatetic philosophy should be the best. Thinking while you sit, or while you kneel with the eyes closed or fixed upon vacancy, the mind lapses into dreams; images of things remote and miscellaneous are merged in the haze of memory, in which facts and fancies roll together almost indistinguishably, and you revert to the vegetative state, voluminous and helpless. Thinking while you walk, on the contrary, keeps you alert; your thoughts, though following some single path through the labyrinth, review real things in their real order; you are keen for discovery, ready for novelties, laughing at every little surprise, even if it is a mishap; you are careful to choose the right road, and if you take the wrong one, you are anxious and able to correct your error. Meantime, the fumes of digestion are dissipated by the fresh air; the head is cleared and kept aloft, where it may survey the scene; attention is stimulated by the novel objects constantly appearing; a thousand hypotheses run to meet them in an amiable competition which the event soon solves without ambiguity; and the scene as a whole is found to change with the changed station of the traveller, revealing to him his separate existence and his always limited scope, together with the distinction (which is all wisdom in a nutshell) between how things look and what they are.

A naturalist who was also a poet might describe the summer and winter tours of all the animals—worms, reptiles, fishes, birds, insects, and quadrupeds—telling us what different things they travel to see or to smell, and how differently they probably see and smell them. A mere moralist is more cramped in his sympathies and can imagine only human experience. And yet, when once the biped has learned to stand firmly on his hind legs, the human mind, more agile if less steady than a camera on its tripod, can be carried nimbly to any eminence or *Aussichtsthurm;* and if the prospect is unpleasing, it can scamper down again and perhaps change its chance environment for a better one. It is not the eye only that is consulted in surveying the panorama, and choosing some striking feature or hill-top for the end of the journey. The eye knows very well that it is only a scout, a more dignified substitute for the nose; and most of the pleasures it finds are vicarious and a mere promise of other satisfactions, like the scent of game. A search for the picturesque is the last and idlest motive of travel. Ordinarily the tribes of men move on more pressing errands and in some distress.

The most radical form of travel, and the most tragic, is migration. Looking at her birthplace the soul may well recoil; she may find it barren, threatening, or ugly. The very odiousness of the scene may compel her to conceive a negative, a contrast, an ideal: she will dream of El Dorado and the Golden Age, and rather than endure the ills she hath she may fly to anything she knows not of. This hope is not necessarily deceptive: in travel, as in being born, interest may drown the discomfort of finding oneself in a foreign me-

dium: the solitude and liberty of the wide world may prove
more stimulating than chilling. Yet migration like birth is
heroic: the soul is signing away her safety for a blank cheque.
A social animal like man cannot change his habitat without
changing his friends, nor his friends without changing his
manners and his ideas. An immediate token of all this, when
he goes into a foreign country, is the foreign language which
he hears there, and which he probably will never be able to
speak with ease or with true propriety. The exile, to be
happy, must be born again: he must change his moral climate
and the inner landscape of his mind. In the greatest migration of our time, that of Europeans to America, I know by
observation how easily this may be done, at least in the second generation; but a circumstance that makes the transformation easy is this: there need be no direct conversion of
mind or heart, or even of language, but only an insensible ex-
change of old habits for new, because the new are more eco-
nomical and soon seem easier. The adaptation, like all the
creative adaptations of nature, is imposed by external influences, by compulsory material arrangements, by daily absorp-
tion in the prevalent forms of thrift and management, and
yet it seems to come from within. The old habits may thus be
soon shed completely and without regret. Colonists, who
move in masses into lands which they find empty or which
they clear of their old inhabitants, have this advantage over
straggling immigrants worming their way into an alien society: their transformation can be thorough and hearty, because
it obeys their genuine impulses working freely in a new material medium, and involves no mixture of incompatible tra-

ditions. America is a vast colony, and it still seems such to
people who migrate even into those prosperous parts of it,
like the United States or the Argentine, which have long-
established constitutions and manners. The newcomers make
themselves at home; they adapt themselves easily and gladly
to the material environment, and make a moral environment
of their own on that solid basis, ignoring or positively con-
demning the religion and culture of the elder Americans.
Perhaps the elder Americans are assimilated in spirit to the
new ones more readily than the new Americans to the old. I
do not mean that any positively German, Italian, Jewish, or
Irish ingredients are incorporated into American traditions:
on the contrary, the more recent immigrants are quick—
much quicker than the British colonists were—to shed all their
memories and start afresh, like Adam in paradise: and for
that very reason they stand out as naked Americans, men
sharply and solely adapted to the present material conditions
of the world: and in this sense their Americanism is louder
and bolder than that of the old Yankees or the old Southern-
ers, to whom the merely modern world seems perhaps a little
deafening and a little unprincipled.

Compared with the emigrant the explorer is the greater
traveller; his ventures are less momentous but more dashing
and more prolonged. The idea of migration is often latent in
his mind too: if he is so curious to discover new lands, and to
describe them, it is partly because he might not be sorry to
appropriate them. But the potential conqueror in him is often
subdued into a disinterested adventurer and a scientific observer. He may turn into a wanderer. Your true explorer or

naturalist sallies forth in the domestic interest; his heart is never uprooted; he goes foraging like a soldier, out in self-defence, or for loot, or for elbow room. Whether the reward hoped for be wealth or knowledge, it is destined to enrich his native possessions, to perfect something already dear: he is the emissary of his home science or home politics. Your rambler, on the contrary, is out on the loose, innocently idle, or driven by some morbid compulsion; his discoveries, if he makes any, will be lucky chances, to be attributed to sheer restlessness and fishing in troubled waters. The inveterate wanderer is a deluded person, trying like the Flying Dutchman to escape from himself: his instinct is to curl up in a safe nook unobserved, and start prowling again in the morning, without purpose and without profit. He is a voluntary outcast, a tramp. The maladaptation from which he suffers and which drives him from society may not be his fault: it may be due to the closeness of the home atmosphere, the coldness there, the intolerable ache of discords always repeated and right notes never struck. Or it may express an idiosyncrasy by no means regrettable, a wild atavistic instinct, or a mere need of stretching one's legs, or a young impulse to do something hard and novel. The mountain-climber, the arctic explorer, the passionate hunter or yachtsman, chooses his sport probably for mixed reasons: because he loves nature; because having nothing to do he is in need of exercise and must do something or other; or because custom, vanity, or rivalry has given him that bent; but the chief reason, if he is a genuine traveller for travel's sake, is that the world is too much with us, and we are too much with ourselves. We need sometimes to escape into open solitudes, into aimlessness, into the moral holiday of running some pure hazard, in order to sharpen the edge of life, to taste hardship, and to be compelled to work desperately for a moment at no matter what.

In the wake of the explorer another type of traveller is apt to follow, the most legitimate, constant, and normal of all: I mean the merchant. Nowadays a merchant may sit all his life at a desk in his native town and never join a caravan nor run the risk of drowning; he may never even go down into his shop or to the ship's side to examine or to sell his wares. This is a pity and takes half the humanity and all the poetry out of trade. If a merchant may be sedentary, it should be at least in one of those old mansions in Amsterdam where the ships came up the canal to the master's door, and the bales of merchandise were hoisted into the great lofts at the top of his house by a pulley that, like a curious gargoyle, projected from the gable. There the comforts and good cheer of family life could be enjoyed under the same roof that sheltered your wealth and received your customers. But if the merchant now will not travel, others must travel for him. I know that the commercial traveller is a vulgar man, who eats and drinks too much and loves ribald stories; he, like his superior, has been robbed of his natural dignity and his full art by the division of labour, the telegraph, and the uniformity of modern countries and modern minds; nevertheless I have a certain sympathy with him, and in those provincial inns where he is the ruling spirit, I have found him full of pleasant knowledge, as a traveller should be. But commerce has also its seafaring men, its engineers, its surveyors, its hunters and its trappers: all indefatigable travellers and knowers of the earth. My own parents belonged to the colonial official classes, and China and Manila, although I was never there, were familiar names and images to me in childhood; nor can I ever lose the sense of great distances in this watery globe, of strange amiable nations, and of opposed climates and ways of living and thinking, all equally human and legitimate. In my own journeys I have been enticed by romantic monuments and depth of historical interest rather than by geographical marvels; and yet what charm is equal to that of ports and ships and the thought of those ceaseless comings and goings, by which our daily needs are supplied? The most prosaic objects, the most common people and incidents, seen as a panorama of ordered motions, of perpetual journeys by night and day, through a hundred storms, over a thousand bridges and tunnels, take on an epic grandeur, and the mechanism moves so nimbly that it seems to live. It has the fascination, to me at least inexhaustible, of prows cleaving the water, wheels turning, planets ascending and descending the skies: things not alive in themselves but friendly to life, promising us security in motion, power in art, novelty in necessity.

The latest type of traveller, and the most notorious, is the tourist. Having often been one myself, I will throw no stones at him; from the tripper off on a holiday to the eager pilgrim thirsting for facts or for beauty, all tourists are dear to Hermes, the god of travel, who is patron also of amiable curiosity and freedom of mind. There is wisdom in turning as often as possible from the familiar to the unfamiliar: it keeps the mind nimble, it kills prejudice, and it fosters humour. I do not think that frivolity and dissipation of mind and aversion from one's own birthplace, or the aping of foreign manners and arts are serious diseases: they kill, but they do not kill anybody worth saving. There may be in them sometimes a sigh of regret for the impossible, a bit of pathetic homage to an ideal one is condemned to miss; but as a rule they spring not from too much familiarity with alien things but from too little: the last thing a man wishes who really tastes the savour of anything and understands its roots is to generalise or to transplant it; and the more arts and manners a good traveller has assimilated, the more depth and pleasantness he will see in the manners and arts of his own home. Ulysses remembered Ithaca. With a light heart and clear mind he would have admitted that Troy was unrivalled in grandeur, Phaeacia in charm, and Calypso in enchantment: that could not make the sound of the waves breaking on his own shores less pleasant to his ears; it could only render more enlightened, more unhesitating, his choice of what was naturally his. The human heart is local and finite, it has roots: and if the intellect radiates from it, according to its strength, to greater and greater distances, the reports, if they are to be gathered up at all, must be gathered up at that centre. A man who knows the world cannot covet the world; and if he were not content with his lot in it (which after all has included that saving knowledge) he would be showing little respect for all those alien perfections which he professes to admire. They were all local, all finite, all cut off from being anything but what they happened to be; and if such limitation and such arbitrariness were beautiful there, he has but to dig down to the principle of his own life, and clear it of all confusion and indecision, in order to bring it too to perfect expression after its kind: and then wise travellers will come also to his city, and praise its name.

TOWERS

IT IS HARD to be austere gracefully, yet such is the function
of towers; and if they so seldom fulfil it, the reason is, perhaps, that art alone cannot achieve the miracle: it must be a
gift of nature, of the circumstances and conditions imposed
upon art. Most towers, which in our day are useless, are designed on paper to be merely decorative, the consequence
being that they are conventional and trivial, since it is commonly only under the spur of necessity that men do anything
new or solid. Some useless towers are indeed designed to look
austere, but they are merely ugly. The artist cannot be too absolutely consecrated to harmony, to purity, to perfection; the
element of rude strength comes to him best from the theme
which nature forces upon him, from his materials, from the
tragedy of manhood in himself; not from his voluntary art. I
remember a hideous monument to Bismarck at Hamburg: a
heap of boulders trembling upwards into a sort of shaggy
tower, or rough lighthouse, and gradually turning into the

belaboured breast, the ponderous jaw and the threatening eyebrows of the old chancellor. Evidently the intention was to represent him as part and crown of the eternal rock, and to warn the fates, if they ever sought to undo his work, that (as the Germans delicately put it) they would be biting granite. Doubtless today the monstrosity continues to stand there, still new in its insolence and already obsolete in its boasts.

Strength and severity are requisite in a perfect work, but they should lie beneath the surface, in its skeleton or action; and then the delicacy of the expression will make that energy noble. The treatment is like a lady taking her partner's arm; it may proclaim that strength by leaning upon it frankly, but at the same time may control it, and subdue it to pleasant courses; or the ornament may add itself in a sort of despairing contrast, like a garland on a grave. For instance, if military exigencies had demanded a genuine tower in that part of Hamburg, which would have looked strong because it was and needed to be strong, I can imagine a marble medallion of Bismarck let into the midst of that vast plain wall; I should then have liked both the ponderous mass of matter, and the ironic mind that could inhabit and wear it without losing its own fineness.

Somewhat in this fashion the Florentines seem to have intended the rakish tower of their Palazzo Vecchio. It frowns, because that is its official business, being a sentinel on guard: but it also laughs, because the sentinel is young, nimble and gay, and finds it great sport to be perched so high in the blue air. The challenge comes with elegance, in the fashionable phrases; even with a little bravado. The tower is poised a little beyond the wall, on the edge of the projecting battlements, like a mocking watchman leaning out of a bastion; and how slender it is in its severity, how gallant in its boldness; and towards the summit, when its police duty is done, how gladly it turns into a belfry, an ornament, a flourish! How cheery this man-at-arms is in his arrogant pose, with feathers above his helmet, light in his eye, and a thin rapier flashing in his deft hand!

Towers in a modern town are a frill and a survival; they seem like the raised hands of the various churches, afraid of being overlooked, and saying to the forgetful public, Here I am! Or perhaps they are rival lightning rods, saying to the emanations of divine grace, Please strike here! But I am afraid grace is not so easily conducted, nor mortals led. In the country, with but one church to each village, towers are not ridiculous. They are the apex of all the roofs huddled about them, and at a distance they are a beacon and a guide to the rambler, who sees them peeping over the shoulder of a hill or a clump of trees; all the charms of nature cannot obliterate the sweetness of living in a Christian country, nor the comfort of it: for before you reach the church you will probably pass an inn, and stop there. As for the office of church towers in being belfries, it is an accident: bells can be hung just as well in a pierced wall, roofed with a bit of thatch: or if your architecture is too grand for that, you can place them in graceful arches, crowned with some aerial ornament: this is the natural adjunct to any Christian church or monastery, since bells came into use. But towers have no more to do with churches than with temples: they are essentially military.

They were naturally added to palaces and to other town buildings when they tended to become castles. Wherever a treasure was kept or a leader resided, the house had to be fortified: and this may happen again, when nations fight no more, because they have disappeared, and only civil war survives. I imagine church-towers too were originally for defence, the consequent strength of the walls making them suitable to hang the bells in; so that their upper part sometimes became a sort of dove-cot, from which peals issued instead of doves. Still they were no essential part of the church edifice, and usually stood by themselves at a little distance. It was later, in the palmy days of mediaeval exuberance, that pyramids of galleries and pinnacles, or fretted spires, or jaunty lanterns were raised over the nave or the aisles of churches. Otherwise the tower, even if contiguous to the body of the church, rose from its own foundations, perhaps forming a porch, the better to protect the entrance. Even now, it seems sometimes that full-length towers are the most beautiful, or at least the best remembered.

In Florence itself the campanile of Giotto is a masterpiece in design and a marvel in decoration; yet it seems like an inlaid box, or enlarged jewel, and even in its structure it resembles too much an architect's model, designed for the sake of designing. Lucky that architects are not magicians, but have to struggle with matter and with employers: if they could execute everything they dream of, their works would be monstrous or trivial. The preciousness of Giotto's masterpiece is too pervasive; that initial austerity, so necessary for supreme beauty, is too much obscured: had it stood more plainly behind these graces, to stiffen and distribute them, it might have turned this beauty into grandeur. To me—and I confess it may be an accident of temperament—beauty implies reserve: not only the reserve of good taste (which of course the campanile has), not only the reserve of disdain (which perhaps it has too), that disdain which in all Greek beauty is so conspicuous: but also the reserve of sorrow, of denial, of death foreseen and accepted and only hidden for a moment, as it were, in the sheath of life. I know that death too is but a sheath, from which life is drawn flashing always afresh: but the secret of this alternation is that neither life nor death is substantial, and that both must be accepted with a profound reserve, because they are both deceptive.

For this reason I prefer a tower with more substance in it, more a product of accident and of profound forces, the Giralda of Seville. It is fundamentally a tower of defence, part of the great enclosure which once held the mosque, the Alcazar, and the city; it is enormous, simple, windowless to a considerable height. Yet, where the openings begin, the wall too receives a decorative touch: the surface is fretted and divided into long panels; and the windows themselves are graced with little pillars, and mouldings and lobes. As for the original part, the Saracenic foundation is a great square bastion hardly differing from any other, save that within it ran the inclined plane on which the Moorish chivalry might ride up to the walls, and inspect their dominion without dismounting.

HELLENISM AND BARBARISM

HERODOTUS, the books of whose history are named after the nine Muses, does not hesitate to represent the Persian Wars as an episode in an epic conflict between Europe and Asia. The headspring of it was the rape of Europa (who was an Asiatic) by the amorous Jove. The rape of Helen was the retort courteous on the part of Asia to that compliment: and I am not sure that we are not invited to look forward to an endless chain of abductions and punitive expeditions, in which only some old beauty without virtue may be recovered at the price of rivers of young men's blood.

What was Europe and what was Asia? Anything more than parts of the same earth separated by the Hellespont? Since the Muses inspired the narrative, I will suppose that they were wrapping in their myth some eternal oracle. Perhaps we may catch a first hint of their meaning if instead of

This essay appeared in *Greek Heritage: The American Quarterly of Greek Culture* I (Winter 1963).

Europe we said Hellas, and instead of Asia, Babylon. Hellas was not a limited land: it lay on both sides of the Hellespont. Troy itself was a Hellenic city, and Hellas still extends to every nation where the Gods of Greece are honored without being named, by all men who have attained to self-knowledge. Babylon, too, is everywhere: the tower that was to reach to heaven has been begun in many styles of ambitious architecture, and many times the work has been abandoned because of a confusion of tongues, and the inevitable collapse of a will that has no necessary roots in nature. The eternal conflict between Hellas and Babylon will then embody the moral difference between art and adventure, between experience and presumption.

This conflict is not between equals, but between an elder power and a younger hope, between mother and child. Yet in this instance it is not the child that represents adventure and the mother experience: on the contrary, the child only has self-knowledge and foresight, the mother being a primitive divinity, an incorrigible earth-power, blindly weaving her meshes, and blindly bearing her children. In her blindness and obstinacy she is more broadly based and more deeply rooted in nature than her dapper child, and she will survive him. Indeed, he exists, even during his short life, only by partaking in her hard instincts. Without Presumption, who could begin to live at all? The claim to live is the greatest, at bottom the only, Insolence. And as for Adventure, what could there be more hazardous and uncharted than the attempt to establish anything perfect, anything immortal? Is not trust in reason but a new kind of folly? Not, indeed, from the standpoint of Babylon; because this vaulting ambition may be as frank, as tempting, and as glorious as any other, when the wind blows in that direction. But reason would be folly indeed, if folly were not courageously accepted as the synonym of life.

The place of Art is within Impulse, a method in madness, and an adjustment of careful means to an end arbitrary or unattainable. Hellas could never have been a self-sufficient and independent power: its arts, its ships, its gods, its letters all come out of Asia: and its philosophy, so long as it remained noble and unsophisticated, was a transcription of the philosophy of Asia by a more thrifty and modest hand. Europa was a child of Asia, of the same race and nature. An animal life can never be transplanted into a heaven of logic; and reason becomes impossible if the basis of reason, which is passion, has been removed. The glory of Hellas is rather to embody a passion so keen as to burn into a pure light. A sluggish life may endure through all sorts of contradictions and gropings; but as life becomes intense, it must find its center, rub away its excrescences, and in its rapid revolution polish itself until it shines, and sing as it dances.

On the other hand, on the basis of a humanity essentially barbaric, and by a genuine allegiance to the animal in man, reason may hope to establish a perfect domination: the obstacles to it are physical and accidental, not logical. Hellas must accept (as Greece did most heartily, until the decadence) the pathos and hardships of mortality: blindness, arrrogance, passion, war; it must accept the conditions that at once necessitate and punish these impulses; and having accepted these hard things openly, it will study the means of establishing a frank and magnificent harmony out of these fated elements.

How will the regimen of reason and art, established by the Hellenic legislator, differ from a barbarous life of adventure? Not in its source, which is animal economy; not in its motive power, which is animal will: but in its steadiness and scope, in its self-knowledge. Barbaric poets may now sing war and now the chase, now love or a mystic philosophy: but the Hellenic sage will survey and define the actual conditions of human nature, its scope, and its healthful satisfactions, not excluding angrily any of the idols worshiped by the barbarian, but putting them where they belong. This understanding of reason is itself an adventure—that fact must not be denied for a moment: it is a hope embraced instinctively, as any passion embraces any hope, and it runs a grave risk of failure—perhaps total, almost certainly partial. It presumes a certain constancy in the world and in human nature. This constancy can hardly be absolute, the flux of things is too deep and pervasive for that; but in so far as a constancy exists, sufficient to justify moral philosophy, the attitude of a sheer adventurer becomes repulsive: it is folly to wait for successive moments to suggest successive actions, as is done by wild animals and the romantic man. Don Quixote, throwing the reins on the neck of Rosinante, is the perfect adventurer. If he had been a bit of protoplasm floating in a tepid sea, what else could he have done? But his case was far otherwise: he was mounted and armed, so that behind his romantic nescience lay the arts of horsemanship and war. His romanticism is archaic, an atavism in the midst of civilization: he is not like Faust or Peer Gynt, ready for anything and craving to see and to do all that is possible. He wishes to right wrongs, to defend the outraged and rescue the oppressed. He does not conceive, like those essential barbarians, that man has a vague soul to develop *ad libitum:* on the contrary, he is sure that he, and other men, have definite souls to save, that is, to rescue from adverse circumstances and to surround by other circumstances that may bring them to perfection and happiness. Therefore the romanticism of Don Quixote is a madness, an accident; not like that of barbarians a beginning of experience that, with time, might lead to the discovery of nature and art. Goethe, if not Faust or Peer Gynt or Ibsen, made this discovery, and became "classical": but I am afraid a retrospective classicism is not genuine, but only a phase of romanticism: true classicism is the understanding that life is an art within natural limits. The genuine romantic is hard to convert, because he has not been false to his nature by accident, but has not yet a nature to which to be true. Don Quixote, on the contrary, can be converted; and it was profoundly just and consistent in Cervantes to represent him on his deathbed confessing his error, and reverting to common sense and sane religion. He was a civilized soul infected with barbarism; and his romantic folly was but a superficial misdirection of his natural reason and goodness.

Faust and Peer Gynt, on the contrary, were barbarians infected with civilization. It may be, for such natures, a real corruption and dishonor, like the taming of a wild animal. Such souls cannot be truly reformed or converted: they are always looking forward for the next chance of being earnestly foolish. The trappings of civilization, though they may wear them easily for a time, will before long be discarded as chains, or despised as frills and periwigs; and the reason is that these men have no belief in a divine world about them or in a settled nature in themselves. They think that what they feel determines what they are and what they shall be: they wish to command fortune, and this overbearing courage they call freedom, as if a man were freer in wanting what he wants than in being what he is. In reality, nature is as much nature in creating their wishes as in establishing their destiny; and all this pother of barbarism is a vast misunderstanding. That fine flush of youth in their souls is not less beautiful or less hopeful for being normal, and having a natural future before it, and an ancient meaning in the cycle of things: their verbal and mental illusions are not the important part of their own inspiration: they are its childish and foolish part, but there is a genuine reality supporting their courage. This is adumbrated in barbaric feeling and in barbaric institutions; and it lends its depth to barbaric philosophy, when this emancipates itself from its civilized masters and becomes autonomous. This genuine reality is Chaos: that nebulous flux of substance in which worlds and souls are formed and dissolved incessantly, though the rate of change be slow in their own eyes, and their lives long. This Chaos is not merely a beginning of existence, or its point of departure: it is there always, in "the waters that are under the earth." A subtle and profound mutation runs through all things; and presently the names thereof know them no more. It is to this Chaos that the barbaric soul responds nobly, and is deeply adjusted: it is deeper in its formlessness and courageous despair than the civilized soul in its artful nest.

Not that the civilized soul has not its own superiority, in that it can escape from the flux altogether, in allegiance though not in fate, and can regard with equanimity the further drift of existence, as the sailor in port regards the storm. But this superiority of the rational soul lies in another direction, which for the barbarian is not appreciable. In respect to the forces that confront the barbarian, and the drift of things in which he is wholly immersed, his attitude is the only honest one. If we hug existence, let us hug it as it is, and not its false image: let us set the value of life in the wind that vivifies it, the exhilaration, the terror of willing bravely, whether the attainable or the unattainable: because it is not the possession of any earthly thing that is long possible or valuable, but only the joy of winning something that is soon to be thrown away.

Such is the attitude of experimental living, and life is at bottom always an experiment. It is the sole attitude possible to animals who have no real dwellings, but only the habit of not lying down anywhere before turning round several times and thoroughly stamping down their experimental bed. But few men are so simple: I am not sure of the existence of innocent savages, subject to some wild fears or frolics, but unharassed by any proud determination to be adventurous, cruel, and lordly at any cost. Most men, if not all, are sophisticated; and the barbarian in particular has weapons and a sense of honor. He is very exacting in the family; perhaps sacrifices his first-born, and performs the most arduous and painful ceremonies, because it is the custom to do so. He is the slave of tradition, which with him is only *hereditary fashion,* and, though arbitrary, difficult to change: it is not *hereditary art,* since it is not exercised upon matter for the benefit of spirit, but arises only by some freak of fancy, and is thereafter imposed on spirit by physical pressure and contagion.

NOTE ON GOETHE'S *CHORUS*

MYSTICUS IN FAUST

Alles Vergängliche ist nur ein Gleichnis;
Das Unzulängliche, hier wird's Ereignis,
Das Unbegreifliche, hier wird's gethan;
Das Ewig-Weibliche zieht uns hinan.

GOETHE had large sympathies and varied intuitions; we must not be surprised if his ultimate conceptions are eclectic and their mutual relations vague. It is perhaps only this vagueness that he takes for an ultimate mysticism: in his youth the religion of emotion and peace in *die schöne Seele* had not been unknown to him. He could also be led to a pantheistic mysticism through his cosmology.

That everything transitory—the whole miscellany of nature, history, and mind—is only a likeness or image might be an echo of orthodox Platonism: only Ideas are eternal and existence imperfectly mirrors them in passing. But we are told at

once that here, in this mystical world, the Inadequate generates the Actual, the Event: whereas a Platonist would say the
opposite, that the actual or transitory (what could be more
throughly transitory than an event?) is an inadequate copy
or instance of some perfect Idea. The inadequacy, he would
say, is not in the Idea but in the momentary mirror of existence that reflects yet betrays that Idea. If the event is the adequate reality, the Inadequate that is said to beget it must be
rather the previous events or the flowing substance that, by
their confluence, have brought that event about. Yet how can
the natural antecedents that actually bring a thing about be
inadequate to do so? They are physically, empirically adequate: if they can be called inadequate it must be in a logical
or moral sense, in that while they suffice in fact to produce
the event they do not suffice to *explain* it to our wondering
minds. But why should events explain themselves to our
minds? It is our minds, that when summoned before the
tribunal of events, might be called upon to explain their
uncalled-for demands and presuppositions. If this were what
the *Chorus Mysticus* was intending to say, it should not be
called a mystical but a pragmatist choir.

The remaining lines, however, confirm the impression that
the notions of transiency and of similitude evoked at the beginning have nothing to do with the burden of the whole,
and that we are in a physical universe, celebrating the natural
movement and self-realisation of things. As a synonym, apparently, of the Inadequate, we next come to the Incomprehensible, which nevertheless happens or is done: and we may
recall the famous words of Faust in regard to what must

have been the primary reality: not the Word, nor the Idea, nor the Force, but the Deed. The Deed, though it was at the beginning, essentially issues from something prior and debouches into something ulterior: it must, then, have issued from other deeds and led to more deeds in the future. The Incomprehensible is no doubt the existence of this movement and perhaps also the connection between its phases: although here again there would be intellectual arrogance in *complaining* that reality should be incomprehensible, when it moves so fruitfully without our leave.

Why should it be without our leave, and why should we complain when we are ourselves an integral part of that universal incomprehensibility and inadequacy? No: we do not complain: the Eternal Feminine allures us, and we are ready to be drawn onwards for ever from deed to deed, from event to event; and the notion that all this is only an image of something else, because it is transitory, would seem needless and even perverse; unless indeed we only meant that while the single events are transitory, the chain of them is perpetual, and each moment is but a happy note in an endless symphony. To this I see no possible objection, except that it is not true.

THE SOUL AT PLAY

SO LONG AS parents and nurses, and the general benevolence of mankind, ward off the dangers of life from children, children may play: they may devote their free little minds to imaginary adventures. Playing is dreaming awake; it preserves the strange faculty which gave birth to mythology, the faculty of substituting fancy for fact, without in the least obscuring or confusing actual perceptions. At the prompting of some stray instinct or chance association, you will invent delightful or fearsome circumstances, identifying them, with the most shameful doubleness, with the real ones, which you did not cease to observe and to act upon: you will burst into passionate eloquence, or pant in the direst predicament, all for the fun of it, or rather by virtue of a terrible inner compul-

This essay was composed during the First World War, when Santayana was residing in England. As he has written "Soliloquies in England" in red ink at the top of the holograph, it was originally intended for the volume of that name; but he either mislaid it or reserved it for some other book. [D.C.]

sion; and this dream which is byplay, or play which is a waking dream, will exhibit your brooding soul, if not always to moral advantage or with much coherence, at least in its unsuspected ingenuities of invention. What brilliant images, what subtle emotions, what dramatic turns in the argument of a dream, and in the make-believe of children! You seem to dictate and to compose your fiction deliberately, rejecting, foreseeing, feeling the oncoming revolution towards which circumstances must be addressed: and yet all seems to be dictated and imposed upon you by an unfathomable fatality, by a nature which, since you have no terms in which to conceive its operation, you can only call inspiration or fate. In this play or dream we often hesitate between alternatives; we choose one interpretation of the facts; we construct plots, and enlarge or transmute the stage-setting, to suit the wonderful surprises that (we half-feel) are coming: and we are mightily in earnest in our fine and terrible speeches. In all this we do not express our waking feelings; on the contrary, we seem to flout them, and to try to show how different we might easily and gladly have been from what, alas, we are. The whole world is relaxed and enriched; it is not made better, far from it; to live in mindfully and to live in long, the real world is better than the coloured chaos of dreams, of art, and play, and religion, and utopias: but we have nevertheless a malicious pleasure in flouting nature, and appealing to the deeper chaos of possibility which lies beneath. We want our holiday, we love our midsummer truancies; like shopboys on strike, we put up the shutters in the shop of conscience, and business, and verisimilitude. The cat, the censor, is away, and the mice are having an outing: we are not going to call ourselves to account for any scampering or nibbling of theirs. Yet these silly runaway impulses are parcels of our very selves; truer, in one sense, than the rational self they shatter, which is a sort of mask, a personage it takes much mincing of to render at all presentable. In those mad fragments there is no forced consistency, no systematic suppression, nothing ulterior to live up to; yet there is plenty of spontaneous reasoning and dramatic fiction. We are wandering in the old curiosity shop of the mind, exhibiting its dusty treasures to ourselves as to a stranger, and a rather gullible one: we are setting fancy prices, and telling wonderful tales about everything. Man has an inexhaustible faculty for lying, especially to himself. Soliloquies, I warn the reader, are of all forms of composition the least to be trusted.

Nor is the life of fancy within us suspended when the life of reason, in some measure, supervenes; on the contrary, the workshop of fancy is as busy as ever, not only beneath the varnish of the surface, like the stars shining invisibly by day, but supplying all the warp and woof of our daylight tapestry. It is fancy—the creative reaction of the senses—that supplies the quality of all our perceptions; and fancy supplies even the movement and pattern of all our thoughts, except as comparison or adjustment calls them to book, and renders them coherent, and pertinent to some ulterior issue.

Children play more than grown up people, or seem to play more, because they are more voluble and have less to do; they are not ashamed of their fancies, and have time and humour for indulging them. They can redouble everything they see, and take it for something they do not see, and so instinctive is this reduplication that, when they are at a loss how to make it, they ask eagerly "What is that?" as if they hadn't eyes to see better than their elders. But children are not empiricists; they want to understand, to know what things are *really,* not what they are obviously: they want to know what supplement their dream should add to the data of sense, so as to round off the tale, and know the whole story. And in their play, they readily make these additions and substitutions for themselves, in so far as they have notions out of which to weave their fictions. They will say: "Let us play that this stick is papa and this ball is mama, and that this matchbox is the motor; and that when the motor upsets, mama saves papa's life by rolling out first, so that he falls on top of her, and doesn't hurt himself—and of course *she can't.*" There is not much resemblance in these symbols, nor realism in these events; but this sort of identification of things having only very little in common is current in the mind, and is the condition of signification being found in words or in sensations. Without it we should have remained eternally empiricists, or (to use a shorter Greek word) idiots. Nothing in nature behaves as its sensible essence, if it were substantial and ultimate, might justify it in behaving: everything behaves in a fashion which can only be explained (if explained at all) by a network of subterranean processes, for which that sensible essence is only a symbol of our experience or in our language. Yet in this carnival of disguises and recognitions the soul feels quite at home, for her own life runs beneath the surface; discourse of reason and the stream of images are to her what

the stage-effects and declamation of actors are to the author
of the play—rather disappointing and alien: the inexplicable,
on that level, is the normal. We must sink into the subsoil,
into the network of those vegetative impulses which are the
roots of our being (and which when classified externally we
call the passions) before we can pretend to see how our actions and feelings hang together. The threads which sanity
and science find in the labyrinth of our perceptions are themselves supplied by a dream; we attach particulars to a ghostly
moral unit, like a person, or to a vague imputed motive—jumping at some premonition of what the issue may ultimately
be, and finding in that a reason for whatever may lead up to
it. If the images in perception were the ultimate facts, as empirical philosophy supposes, they would not allow any consec-
utiveness, identity, repetition, or law to subsist at all. But our
images are not the important facts; they are only the stick
and the ball in the children's game. When we said in play
that the stick *was* papa, and the ball *was* mama, we did not
mean what we said: we were indulging in one of those
equivocations about the meaning of the verb *to be* which
philosophers (beginning with Hamlet) have so little suspected. "The stick *is* papa" expresses a substitution, not an
identity. The playful psyche is much more accurately discriminating (as the elaborate grammar of ancient language
shows) than reflective consciousness, as expressed, for instance, in the systems of Locke and Hegel. The psyche is not
at all confused or puzzled when it decided that the stick shall
be *poetically* papa, although *physically* somewhat thinner,
and that the ball shall be officially mama, although *phenome-*

nally somewhat rounder. The spontaneous mind makes no bones of such equivocations, it lives on them; it would be absolutely mad and idiotic if it ever stopped taking the apparent thing for that other thing which is really there. Its first sensations are signals; the absolute image present to sense is not taken for what it literally *is*—nothing in a sane mind is taken literally: to take mental presences literally is not to understand them, it is to be an imbecile. But a healthy child, being quick-witted and no scrupulously artificial empiricist, has no difficulty in taking images poetically and saying that one thing *is* another. And the two natures thus verbally identified, but not logically confused, play together in the vicissitudes of the ensuing drama or game: all the fun of it lies in that; for the stick will make papa behave somewhat after the manner of a stick, and the transubstantiation of the ball into mama will give to the ball (in addition to its rotund accident) all the dignity and humanity of one's softer parent. It would not take much intelligence to cut the stick into small fragments and find out what it is *materially,* and it would take no intelligence at all to insist that papa is papa and can *logically* be nothing else: images are perpetually giving place to other images and things changing into different things. The art of thinking consists in accomplishing these substitutions nimbly, in advance, or in ways that make distant facts rhyme and harmonise together. If images were things, as the idealists try to persuade themselves, we should but need to watch them grow in order to observe and understand the deepest secrets of nature: but images are signs, and happy the man who can interpret them!

That images should be known initially to be signs, before we know what they are signs of, would be a mystery if the human mind were a pure spirit and not, on its mother's side, a child of nature. Certain philosophers, that have no filial piety towards their Mother Psyche, reason as if they were pure spirits, and consequently miss the secret of transitive knowledge, which is a spiritual expression of interaction between bodies. The human spirit is the spirit of a body, the thoughts visiting an animal soul; and consequently its fundamental categories are transcripts of the modes of action and passion proper to an animal living perilously in a material world. Not that the mind itself is not a purely spiritual faculty, or its terms and images not purely ideal presences (they are that taken in themselves, as a poet or logician stopping to peruse them may easily discover); but for the Psyche they are tokens, not pictures interesting in themselves: she reacts and therefore perceives; she understands pragmatically—i.e. knows how to react—before she, or the intellect into which she then passes, begins to contemplate aesthetically or to analyse logically the form of that significant apparition. These signs have intrinsic forms, and are aesthetic realities to which attention may be turned later: but their reality belongs to the realm of essence. Some things will always be true of this reality and others false. It may, for instance, be a green dragon with golden claws; and it would be eternally false of that dragon that it was an angel with violet wings. But the dragon might be a sign, to a physician, of indigestion in the person who saw it, and the angel a sign of inanition: as snakes and pink rats are signs of delirium tremens; and these essences would then enter the world of nature in that capacity, as visionary objects normally called forth at a certain juncture in the life of the psyche.

These natural symbols are not allegories; they are not created expressly to be symbols, in the clear previous presence of what they are to symbolise. Allegories are artificial; they are meant to conceal and enshrine more knowledge than they convey, and to entertain people with the means of expression, as if they were the true object, so that they may not suspect, or may only darkly surmise, that there is a second object behind. Natural symbols, on the contrary, are elements of discovery, beginnings of knowledge; what they signify is not yet known, save as they gradually, by their indications, create an idea of it. They do not, like allegories, serve to hide their object, but like reports to reveal it. When philosophers speak of representative knowledge, they seem to imagine, at times, that nature is like a bad poet, who invents charades to puzzle the mind, and perhaps, if they are clever, to give them the eventual satisfaction of piercing the veil, and having the small excitement of saying to themselves: "I have it! Everybody else is deceived by appearances, but I am blessed with the miraculous gift of divining what appearances, in spite of appearances, really *mean!*" In other words, they think the language of sense is a net of foreign hieroglyphics, that we envisage in the first place as merely decorative flourishes on the heathen face of nature; but that afterwards, through some special initiation by some itinerant missionary, we are surprised to find are also symbols of something ulterior and undreamt of—the life and exploits of the Pharaoh that made them. Of course, it is not impossible that our perceptions should be artificial symbols of this sort, and that a philosopher like Berkeley should be required to tell mankind, when he reached the age of twenty-three, what the experience we had had hitherto, through innumerable centuries, *really meant,* although nobody had suspected it. It is not impossible, but it is foolish: because the symbolism of the senses is of an entirely different kind, as any man of sense can perceive. When a child cries, the cry is a symbol; it signifies not the musical or unmusical sound it intrinsically is, but distress, danger, the need of a mother's attention: and this signification involves the recognition of sources and forms of danger, of causes of distress, such as falls, darkness, solitude, hunger, dampness and pins, which children are exposed to in the natural world. The mother does not need any missionary to come from a far country to tell her that this, and not celestial music, is what her child's crying means. She knows by instinct that the cry is a sign—it is a call; she has but to turn her attention to the quarter from which it sensibly comes to perceive what is the matter. Something in fact is the matter, and that is why the child cries, and why that cry appeals to the mother, by nature predisposed and equipped to remedy that trouble. What the cry *means* is accordingly far better known in the beginning than what the cry *is:* as uneducated people know much better what their words mean than what, philologically or acoustically considered, they actually are.

That there is something ulterior, then, is conveyed to animals by their primitive senses, before reflection discloses to them that there was, as a vehicle for that information, something immediate. Attention is tension; it is expectation. There is little present at first to the animal mind except the direction in which danger or opportunity lies. Every sensation is like the sound of a gun, or the sight of an arm raised to strike a blow. To suppose that in order to know that a signal means something ulterior an animal must first have had experience of that ulterior thing, is a monstrous fallacy of pedants: that is the way knowledge would have been constituted by the philosophers whose systems prove knowledge to be impossible. Nature, however, cares nothing about what dialecticians call possible or impossible, intelligible or unintelligible. She moves (which is impossible according to the most approved logic) and grows (which is unintelligible in terms of discrete discourse). She also thinks, which to philosophers is a mystery. She is prophetic of the future, and prepared for it—another miracle to an understanding that proceeds empirically, and possesses data only of the immediate past, or the immediately receding parts of the flux of nature. From the point of view of nature, however, anticipation is just as easy as retention, and more useful: because organs, if life is to persist, must be pre-adapted to their ulterior functions; and a generic future is therefore more likely to be envisaged by the animal mind than a specific past. Life would be impossible without this pre-adjustment, and the expectation involved; because there would seldom be time, in the actual course of experience, to learn to cope with surrounding things. Indeed, the difficulty goes even deeper; because even if there was plenty of time for education, there would not be a capacity for it, nor a tendency to adaptation unless there was adaptation already, to the extent of being sensitive to the direction in which things lie, and the quarter from which they press upon us, so that a suitable movement may be initiated to draw them in or push them away. Now organs pre-adapted involve (at a certain level, at least) minds forewarned; and it is perfectly possible, in spite of the prejudice of empiricists, to know the future and the absent—of which latter, indeed, the past too is an instance. We may say even more: the absent is the only possible object of knowledge, for intuition of the given is not properly knowledge (in any pregnant sense of the word) but is mere dreaming or thinking. Although the essences given to intuition are always non-existent, positive knowledge is born when these ideal terms are taken as signals only, or manifestations of something substantial which they signify.

The symbol, the sensuous essence given, is not a false flourish, and superfluous for knowledge, as is an artificial allegory, where an honest and plain account of the object was previously at hand, and for all scientific purposes would have been better. An allegory is an occasion for unnecessary perplexity, like a maze in a garden: it is intricacy created for its own sake. But the symbolism native to the mind is like that of an inspired poet, labouring to express, in the truest and deepest way he can, in his own language and rhythms, the burden of his destiny. What is thus immediately reported would be otherwise wholly unknown; until the symbols are multiplied and rendered more accurate, we remain in doubt as to what the object is, further than that the symbol reports and adumbrates it somehow. The sensuous texture of the symbols, like the audible texture of language, is proper to them, not to their object: the nature of the latter therefore remains problematic. The symbols arise, not as copies or intuitions of what they mean, but vegetatively, for their own sweet sake: sensations are the flowers of fancy. Waving there in the midst of much other luxuriance, and being arbitrary and detached, like little dreams, they become entangled, according to their genetic relations, with this or that fact, otherwise describable; and there they *become* symbols for it for reflection, having been *indexes* to those events from the beginning, by virtue of their birth being an index of its conditions. This sensuous symbolism is intrinsically variable, as the affinities of the various symbols it contains are variously felt; it is modified insensibly in sympathy with this or that other image which for a moment it may suggest, or in sympathy with this or that event which it may come to stand for in somebody's experience. "Four-and-twenty blackbirds baked in a pie" is a waif of a notion bred in a day-dream; as it grows it developes dramatically, and fancy adds irresistibly "And when the pie was opened the birds began to sing." The dream thickens, and the dreamer says to himself "How jolly, that!" and presently the machinery behind the dream clicks (for there is always machinery behind the scenes), and inspiration takes a downward turn, and settles comfortably into a more earthly image and a musical coda: "Now wasn't that a dainty dish to set before a King?"

PART II: *Later Essays*

THE BIRTH OF REASON

THIS DISCOVERY that the modern world has missed its way was not due to any special cleverness of mine. In my youth all disinterested spirits were pessimists. I do not refer to vicious or morbid pessimism, which is not disinterested. Being in the dumps may enable a man to shake off conventional hypocrisies and to become an impartial sympathiser with all oppressed races and with the inalienable right of every crying child to cry loudly; but only when speculation has lifted a man from the dumps will he become a disinterested pessimist, like my first guides in free thought, Lucretius, Spinoza, and Schopenhauer. I remember an article about the latter, entitled *Le Bonheur dans le Pessimisme;* and this has been the sort of pessimism to which I assent. I have never seen much evidence of happiness in human life; but personally I cannot complain of my lot. It has been tolerable enough to allow me to be disinterested in speculation and therefore

This essay appeared in *The Southern Review* (Summer 1967).

happy in it, as musicians can be happy in music or mathe-
maticians in mathematics. But as men we are all sad failures.
The world, a blind power, is too much for us, even for a Napoleon or a Goethe. But the same world, as an object of
thought, is a wonderful theme; to understand it, virtually
and mythically, as a man may, is the supreme triumph of life
over life, the complete catharsis. Nonetheless, from the point
of view of the animal in man, the truth remains tragic. An
animal can be confident and brave only if he does not suspect
the truth.

That which fills the soul of a confident and brave animal
instead of the truth is the immediate possibility of action;
and this possibility has two factors: first, a generous or passionate movement within him, assuring him of his power;
and second, the sight of some immediate occasion to exercise
that power victoriously. These two simultaneous intuitions
are normal; they are not usually deceptive; there is almost
certainly some relevant power in him, and some relevant occasion to exercise it in his world. Yet he has no intuition of
the truth. Hidden from him altogether is the result that will
actually ensue, and the change of condition and the change of
heart that will assail the next generation. In man, however,
the animal has become somewhat intelligent. To that extent
he acquires an inkling of these ulterior possibilities or proba-
bilities, and acquiesces in the sobering thought that he must
soon die in any case, and that the social objects that he may
propose to himself in his action will, even if attained, lapse
and disappear in time.

Thus unless he becomes disinterested, and capable of seeing

time under the form of eternity, which is *the truth* about it, he will lose heart, or invent imaginary prospects to hide the truth that he fears to discover.

It is only in so far as a man identifies himself with the intellect in him which has the truth for its object, that he can face the world on equal terms and regard it as essentially an inn at which he halts as if he were a traveller from a distant country. This is only a myth intended to represent the spirit's relation to the world, in so far as it transcends the world in its ideal scope. For the spirit is not really lost in its travels, only lost in its dreams. The intellect which transcends the world ideally is a function of the animal soul genetically; and it is a perfectly natural animal function, like all natural self-transcendence in generation, perception, expectation, and action.

It follows from this animal status of mind that the guest in this myth does not enter the inn with the same free option and entire independence with which the host accepts and entertains him, or perhaps kicks him out. The host is subject of course to natural plagues. Rats may sometimes invade his premises, beggars may crowd at his gate, and foundlings may be impertinently laid on his threshold; but he is willing enough to receive paying visitors and treat them well if they are solvent. As to those conceited intellectuals, who swagger about the place and sniff at everything, professing to be foreigners with superior habits, they are not really strangers but prodigal sons, or truant bastards of servants of his, who have had relatively good luck in their wanderings. In fact they are natives; have never thrived and could never thrive anywhere else; but their minds have travelled and there are some things—possibilities and eventualities—about which they can give their host occasional useful hints—and sometimes they invent extraordinary instruments.

In calling the world my host and myself a guest I am therefore playing with words, for I am not in reality a guest in this world but a small yet integral part of it. Nevertheless the fable expresses, in two degrees, the moral relation between the world and any animal in it that tends to become rational. The first degree of this life of reason is reached by animal life whenever any lesson of experience is applied in action, or any likely facts, not personally observed, are conceived and believed to surround the fleeting moment. The second degree of rationality would be reached, as it can hardly be reached in normal life, if the truth about things so occupied the foreground that the past and future in any episode or in any dramatic situation were felt as clearly as the present; or in other words, if the truth about things absorbed and replaced the successive perception of them. This would be a trance, not incompatible with action, since it is often in the great crises of action that it arises, yet incompatible with the alternate and discursive passage of impressions and ideas in ordinary life.

Now the least touch of rational reflection withdraws the mind from the blindly appetitive and perceptual flux of animal interests, themselves private and crossing the generative flux of the inanimate world. This mental remove gains perspective and may bring as much admiration of the scenes conceived as it does withdrawal from them. Nothing is more

mechanical and self-repeating than the revolution of the earth
and of the other planets; but that, and even more the stars
that for us seem fixed, excite our enthusiastic wonder; and
the spirit is more at home in that order of motions and—as it
seemed to the ancients—that divine life, than in any earthly
business. The notion that mechanized motion is hostile to
reason or the spirit, because it cannot think or love erratically
as men do, is one of those absurdities that render the talking
world, especially in modern times, really foreign and odious
to spirit; since spirit is precisely the voice of order in nature,
the music, as full of light as of motion, of joy as of peace,
that comes with an even partial and momentary perfection in
some vital rhythm. There would therefore be nothing odious
or alien to spirit in the modern world, if our world were me-
chanically perfect and harmonious. The trouble is that its
mechanisms are now utterly disorganised and its impulses
distracted, so that spirit can arise in it only spasmodically, to
suffer and to fail. For just as the birth of spirit is joyous, because some nascent harmony evokes it, so the rending or
smothering of that harmony, if not sudden, imposes useless
struggles and suffering.

The brave natural man who, like a healthy animal, meets
each successive occasion for action with a confident impulse
and an adequate perception of the immediate facts would
evidently lead a life that from his own point of view, and for
his own conscience, would be perfectly satisfying; and the absence of all speculation and of all comprehensive vision of the
truth about his life would not disturb him. He would be living by animal faith, doing at each moment what he felt must

be done, and leaving it to God, if God is interested in the matter, to control the issue and to pass judgement on the actors. It is presumably in this mood that all the lower animals live, without speculation or any conception of the truth, or any wish for such a conception.

It is in this mood that the modern man, in so far as he can discard traditional ideas and institutions, desires to live: he craves a life of pure action, obeying his *essor vital,* doing things as new and as varied as possible, with extreme energy, between a forgotten dead past and an empty unpredictable future. Certainly a free, sporting, romantic ideal of life; and I, not being a dogmatist in morals, cannot blame anybody who honestly entertains or realises it. I only ask to be allowed the same moral liberty that I concede to others; and as my nature happens to be inclined to reflection, I cannot help considering what the history of such a purely impulsive life is likely to be, and actually is.

Let me then suppose that I am the source of my own destiny and may choose at each moment the direction that it shall take. Still a particular field of choices is presented to me without my asking or my leave, and also the particular specious character and magnetic force, at this moment, of a few possibilities: I cannot choose what I do not think of, and I cannot think of everything at once, or compare all values. My "creative" impulse is therefore caught in a fatal predicament, and my freedom flutters in a cage. But perhaps, according to the doctrine of Karma, I have forged the bars that imprison me, and in a former life, when my vision was clearer and wider, I sinfully chose the worthless objects that now obsess me.

Very well: in a myth, a poetic parody of true science, I have now introduced moral order into my romantic egotism. I still profess to be my own creator, but under what terrible inexorable conditions! If I was originally a free spirit, not yet smothered in a world woven by my own folly, how could my first choice, or any of my choices, be a wrong one? In my estimation it must have seemed the best: what authority, not my own will, has dared to intervene and call my good evil? And what utterly alien fatality could endow that illegitimate authority with the cruel power to turn the first good which I embraced into an incubus, and to oblige me for ever afterwards to hate what in my freedom I had loved?

In any case, the boast that my spirit was an absolute power, free from the past and master of the future, now turns out to be a treble illusion: I am not master even of the present, since I am faced with alternatives that I never chose and that perhaps I hate; from which certainly I cannot liberate myself and return to the pristine freedom which, according to the fable I am spinning, I once enjoyed. And even if then I was free and master of the future, how false that old mastery of mine then renders the alleged mastery of my present now! I have limited, loaded, and poisoned my whole future by one momentous decision, and the least use of my freedom makes me thereafter a created, fated, hypnotised thing compelled to hate my own being. Nor finally is it possible for me to escape from this predicament: for though I give orders and exert my will,

I cannot bind myself at the next moment to persevere in my new choice. Did I not boast that I was utterly free? Then the fable that I created my present condition was false; and it is an absolute groundless fatality that at each moment makes me what I am and falsely convinces me that I can turn myself into whatever I choose.

The nightmare of absolute freedom being thus self-destructive, let me return to the sober consideration of spontaneous action as it naturally comes about both in my host, the world, and in that spirit within me that seems to be only a guest there and a critical stranger. My host is proud of being a landlord; he likes to dwell on the particular features of his establishment, the conveniences, the prospect, the wines, the previous distinguished patrons; and if he grumbles at the hard times and at the inconstancy of fashions in public taste, he betrays a comfortable sense of his solid position and assured future. The notion that he might have been a duke, or a sailor or a poet, if it ever crossed his mind in boyhood, never troubles his mind. He means to possess all the virtues of John Bull, with only the becoming limitations. So too, *mutatis mutandis,* all healthy animals would assure us, if they could speak; nor would the stars or the atoms hold a different language, except that it would be even more precise and emphatic. To be anything but what they are, or do anything but what they do, would seem to them inconceivable.

The world, then, both mechanical and social, lives quite at home in its limitations, its habits, and its possibilites. Yet where there is animation (and perhaps even where there is not), the natural impulse of one portion sometimes arrests or diverts the natural impulse of another part; and then the placid exercise of customary motions is broken by a jolt. Perhaps there are long, complicated, inextricable struggles, until death removes the combatants without assuring peace to their successors. The world is therefore at every moment in a state of insecure equilibrium; for the impulses that vivify it are fundamentally many, unitary in a moral or historical sense, as the will of an animal at any moment seems unitary, and is felt by that animal as a vague total compulsion and action: for it is the impulse of a living organism moving as a whole. Yet that organism is a marvellously complex and easily disturbed or dismembered unit, as even what we call atoms turn out to be; and it is only by a precarious interlocking of many elementary tropes that any organism holds together, or works as a practical unit on the large superficial scale of human science or politics.

We may gather from this observation how hidden and remote from the pictorial and dramatic terms of human language are the controlling forces that make existence and health possible to mankind. The first prerequisite to the existence of life is a definite order, a predetermined, difficult, approximate order to be established and preserved in animal and social bodies. Order presupposes a plurality of elements, and therefore a danger of disruption; but no order would tend to arise at all in a manifold of elements unless native to each of these, there was a sensitivity to the presence and affinity of other elements with which it might spontaneously initiate a common movement: a dance maintaining a particular pattern, or maintaining a variable harmony, either chang-

ing the total resulting figure spontaneously or changing it
under stress of some novel external force. Flux and order are
equally necessary to the existence of anything; and the modern talk about the contrast between the static or stagnant and
the dynamic or active vents some local animosity against
some special formation, but shows no insight into the life of
things. Every form, intuited or defined, is for ever what that
intuition or definition specifies and can never change; but any
existing object to which that ideal form is assigned in perception, either never possesses it at all, or possesses it only for an
indivisible and imperceptible instant. No wooden wheel is a
perfect circle; or if by miracle it ever momentarily was one,
changes of tension, temperature, or atomic structure would
even then be in the act of making it not perfectly circular.
Were the wheel simply the perfect circle which by an elaborate process of material stimulation it prompts the mind to
conceive, it would not be a wheel or a part of nature at all,
but only the eternal theme, the circle, which the mind has
distinguished, can retain and can use as a sign, in its thinking, for the very special material instrument which the wheel
is for the body in its animal gropings.

Static or stagnant, then, nothing material can ever be, except to the superficial impatience of some fretful creature that
wants obstinate material Nature to get out of its way. Really
changeless are only the forms that the mind distinguishes in
passing. Dynamic or active in some degree is, on the contrary,
the whole realm of matter, flowing at its own meandering
paces through an endless variety of forms.

SPIRIT IN THE SANCTUARY

THOSE who think of the truth as the sum of what we read in the newspapers or may find in the Encyclopaedia Britannica move sanely enough at one conventional level. Such reports are not ordinarily false. They designate real events, objects truly discoverable on the scale of the human senses; and they trace the relations of these objects and events on the plane of human action. But the form thus assumed by those facts is a mere image. In their aspect and individuality our ideas are signs, not portions, of what exists beyond us; and it is only when experiment and calculation succeed in penetrating beneath the image, that (for instance in mathematical physics) we may gain some more precise, though still symbolic, notion of the forces that surround us. We and our knowledge are a part of nature: it is therefore inevitable that the rest of nature, in its concreteness, should be external to us. We cannot share the full reality that other events carry with them. Absolute

This essay appeared in *American Scholar* (Winter 1963).

truth is hidden from us, and the deeper our science goes, the more ghostly it becomes. In entering that temple we have passed out of the sunlight. We are no longer surrounded by living objects, but by images of the gods.

That to which spirit aspires, initially and indomitably, the full truth and the perfect good, dwells like the gods of Egypt in a dark inner chamber. It can be fitly approached only with downcast eyes and declared only in a half-intelligible liturgy by a priest shorn and purified and clothed in white, reverently treading the ground unshod, and bearing in one hand a flickering lamp and in the other a censer that spreads in puffs a half-translucent sweet-smelling cloud. Legend is such a cloud of incense, science is such a lamp. They reveal secrets and express awe, leaving us acquainted with the unintelligible beauty and terror of things, with some sure measure for them, and some means of propitiating them. In scientific theory we remain, as it were, in the outer hall or narthex of the sacred edifice. Daylight, if not sunlight, continues to flood the scene with an indirect illumination. Sensuous brightness may be gone, but conceptual lucidity is enhanced, and we see more plainly than ever the essential geometrical lines of our pictorial world. The mystery thickens, however, if we are allowed to penetrate further. Soon human categories become inapplicable. We require divine lights, and we find at first no means of obtaining them. The change is somewhat as if, at the opera, the stage was suddenly darkened, the plot of the drama forgotten, the audience and our own persons shut off from consciousness, and only the music continued. We should be living in a perfectly definite medium, in a world of sound which might be studied and explored *ad infinitum* in its own terms; yet in contrast to the human life we had been living before, we should have passed into an abstract sphere; and the analogies and symbolic correspondences would be elusive by which this flood of music might still seem somehow to express the passions of a human soul. So when the religious imagination opens up a theological world, we may have some difficulty in tracing any correspondence between this new dramatic labyrinth and the hard tangle of our daily lives. The profane will say we are dreaming; and we in turn will pity them for living blindly, amid paltry cares, in ignorance of the celestial realities that envelope them on every side.

Yet is is impossible for nature to possess a constitution so recondite that spirit might not match it in variety, explore it thoroughly, and think it as it is. The obstacles to true understanding are accidental only: mind is essentially the faculty of conceiving truth. Certainly a spirit specifically human has a limited range; because spirit, in entering into a man, has taken up a particular station in time and space, and limited itself to the idiom and sensibility of that particular animal. Not so spirit in its essence, which remains capable of entering also into any other animal, and taking up any other point of view. This same power of intuition which in man spreads over a certain region of being, over certain sights, sounds, relations and emotions, if endowed with other organs would spread over other regions of being and light up other pictures.

We should therefore be guilty of blasphemy if, on first seeing into the recesses of the inner temple and finding them dark, we asserted that there was nothing there, no gods and even no recesses. On the contrary, with a little patience, we may begin to see in the dark, to distinguish, I mean, region from region by a new kind of perception, as some animals do by scent, or by instinctive reactions to us incomprehensible. We should then be able to guide our steps through that maze, like the priest with his lamp. And this simile hardly does our case justice; because the invisible regions open to spirit are not confined and increasingly narrowed, like the concentric passages in an Egyptian sanctuary. If science ever proves to be a blind alley, that is only because it thinks in terms of the human senses, terms too gross and summary to express the deeper structure of nature. Essentially, round each sensuous image and each pulse of feeling there opens out for pure intelligence an endless radiation of kindred or of contrasted forms. Where perception ends imagination begins; and far from being smothered or lost in nothingness, spirit is liberated from the continual irrelevance and self-interruption of sensation, and is allowed to deepen apprehension of what has already been revealed. And this store of impressions is no dead treasure; every idea is a seed; and presently a whole garden, a whole forest, springs up out of those few grains of experience.

Dream-pictures, you will say; hallucinations. What have they to do with truth? Nothing, or very little, if you expect the mind to be a transparent medium, or not a medium at all, but a pure intellectual revelation of things as they are. But such is not the nature of consciousness in its rudiments, which are opaque if regarded as knowledge, making an addition—such as pleasure or pain—to their occasions, rather than being a cognition of these occasions. Yet what could be more relevant to its occasion, more significant of eventual things, than the signal of pain or pleasure, suddenly calling the spirit to attention? What could rouse us better to chase our fortunes or unearth the secrets of our own life?

Undoubtedly the spirit, when fed by a vigorous temperament and at the same time liberated from servitude to external things, plays and sings quite fantastically. Yet even then, far as those inner lights may be from showing the true structure of nature, imagination cannot help being truly expressive, as in music, of the secret complexities of life in ourselves. There is no better transcript of those delicate affinities, those responsible motions which are alive in our flesh. Biology and physiology give far cruder and more external renderings of that intricate, pauseful, hereditary play of organic forces which keeps our bodies together, and our minds at work. Pure imagination, sheer emotion, endlessly modulated, are therefore true symbols (though wholly original and nondescriptive in their sensuous essence) for a certain region of the material world, namely, for the internal maturation and flowering of certain animal powers.

There is psychological truth, as in autobiography; also lyric sincerity or the transformation of reality into a world of fable. These two documentary sorts of truth cannot help dogging the steps of even madmen. But play-life in the least critical and most ignorant peoples, as also in children, is never unchecked: if it were, it would kill itself off like a radical disease. The world of fable is continually collated, enriched, interpreted by common knowledge: it is often refined and spiritually transfigured by the wisdom of the prophet or the poet that gives it shape. There then arises a civilised religion, sane in spirit, though necessarily irrational in its primary and deepest texture: for if religion became radically rational it would no longer be religion. But divination, and deepening of human sentiment in solitude, in indifference or possible opposition to the facts of nature, may be combined with common sense by a sort of truce or diplomatic marriage. Convention and reason may be safely established in the lay government of the world, whilst the temple remains standing, honoured if seldom entered; and no priggish effort is made to discredit traditional fables or to drown the oracles that may have come from the unknown in antiquity. Free imagination may be allowed to vegetate in a walled garden, even in the midst of a city where all is thrift, hubbub, mechanism, and exact science.

From this compromise it is only a step to philosophical insight and a rational policy regarding irrational things. We need only reflect on the basis of human imagination and human morality; how immense the extent and complexity of nature, how frail all virtue and all life. I think that, if not the priests of antiquity, at least a future priesthood could be capable of seeing in the dimness of their glittering shrines truths that cannot bear the light of day: not that the light of day would disprove them, but that they, in their tragic horror, would extinguish the light of day in an unchastened spirit.

Such truths must be conveyed with caution. A wise legislator will be guided by them, while leaving them unspoken. If they were rashly published, they would not be believed. The mind of man is necessarily humanistic: not, indeed, in so far as it is pure spirit or intelligence, but in all its initial perspectives and motives. The psyche would be unhinged and her life stopped if she were emancipated, like the spirit, from her animal purposes and asked to live in the light of ultimate truths. *Memento mori* gives only a hint of it. At every step, full knowledge of the conditions, co-presence of the whole past and the whole future, would paralyse impulse; or else would divorce it so completely from reflection that reflection itself would be sterilised and nipped in the bud. This we see continually happening when an ardent young man becomes a man of business or a man of the world. The momentum and the routine of action now forbid him to ask if what he does is worth while. He must be true to his commitments, however false his commitments may be to his true nature. Thus the wheel of fortune keeps turning, to the ruin of all at last.

The darkness of the holy of holies is a protective darkness, not a product of fudge. The spirit needs it as the eye requires the eyelid to relieve and to punctuate its visions, and requires sleep to rest from them altogether and to digest them. If the priests tell you that they have miracle-working relics or secret oracles concealed in the sanctuary, they are speaking in parables without knowing it. They have nothing worth mentioning in the ark or the Kaaba; their consecrated wafer has no magic powers; their holy wells nothing medicinal: yet there is salvation in turning from the world of men and of words into that darkness and silence. In the sanctuary the spirit renews its youth, shakes off its cruel obsessions like a bad dream, reasserts its indomitable affinities with things not human, and learns to return to its earthly life no longer a slave, no longer altogether a fool, but conscious of the invisible deity for whom all these are little troubles, punishments sent without anger, and false promises that, in our deepest being, we do not wish had been true.

NATURAL AND ULTIMATE

RELIGION

WHY DO men possess a religion at all? For two reasons, and on two levels. The first reason, on the level of natural life, is that we are all committed, without our previous consent, to the enterprise of living. We are all engaged more or less prosperously in obeying habits, impulses, affections, and hopes. We feel a more or less kindred effort animating all nature and especially a certain portion of mankind, those, namely, who are of our race, or of our way of thinking. Yet since even with this support, success in any project is doubtful, and even the interpretation of our own wills often uncertain, we are prone to imagine a God, more powerful and more friendly than our human neighbours, more powerful and friendly even than the ordinary course of nature, who shall abet us in our hazardous enterprise and assure us of ultimate

This essay appeared in *National Review* (December 31, 1963).

success. Such is the first origin and function of human religion: it arises in a mind sure of its purposes but incapable of carrying them out unaided: it is the appeal of the animal soul to heaven for help, for guidance, for vengeance; the comfort found in the hope that such aid is possible, and thankfulness poured out when, somewhat exceptionally, such aid seems actually to come.

I will not say—though it would be plausible—that this natural religion is vain. Let me admit, since I am admitting all material possibilities, that co-operative and sympathetic deities hover above us, prompting and sanctioning our moral life. If not the literal fact, that ancient assurance is at least a good poetic symbol for the natural or supernatural forces by which the spirit is actually supported—generative and protective forces in the first instance and in many respects, yet treacherous forces in the end, ultimately requiring the supreme sacrifice of all that we naturally love: not only a death for each individual life, but a fatal collective failure and collapse for every collective success. No: I do not think the spirit need trouble to quarrel with traditional religion, ancient or modern, mythological or scriptural. The spirit is essentially a poet, and must be tender to its own works. Are they not full of the truth of experience, cast into such terms as the spirit found at hand? Without carping at traditional faith, I will say this: The enterprise of life, in its natural, animal, political forms, is the basis of science and morality and the public arts: but it is utterly irreligious. Life is a spontaneous, crude, ignorant ambition: a blind self-assertion big with every sort of self-contradiction, agony, and crime. It is precisely that from which a veritable religion would come to redeem us. Those apparently friendly forces to which the nations pray, those imperial gods if they were conscious and moral beings, what would they think of themselves? Who would they say that they were? Would they never wonder where they came from, why such particular thoughts and purposes animated them in creating and governing the universe, and why they had chosen man, or some race, or some type of man—for their particular favourites? What good would they conceive to come of it all? What security would they have for the future? Might not some other playful Titan, some other imperial god, some sudden Napoleon of the heavens, come to upset their thrones, and establish himself and his own family in their place? The new domination might not last, but never would the old domination be again safely restored. Would they not feel like poor men the universal reign of insecurity and ignorance, of helplessness disguised by romantic swagger, creeping like a cold mist into the marrow of their bones? Yes; and even without any external enemies or visible dangers, might not the mood of a divine life gradually change of itself, like the weather? Might it not turn from zephyrs to storm, from storm to silence? Might not the universal Titan find himself suddenly fertile with a surprising brood, as a tree puts forth leaves or an animal has young: and might not all his watchfulness and industry on behalf of his litter turn out useless in the end, might not all his children die, might not his own affection and sorrow grow weary and dreamlike, and might he not relapse into an uneasy solitude, haunted by persistent memories and by the shadow of a future, perhaps horrible and certainly unforeseen? Surely, for Titans and men, for nations and doctrines, such is inevitably the enterprise of life; and if we look to any god that shares that enterprise, we look to nothing that, except by accident, is at all wiser or stronger than ourselves. If we are the creatures of some cosmic Demiurgus, of some romantic artist playing with atoms and with rays of light, surely nobody ever stood in greater need than that deity of repentance and liberation. Great or small, recent or ancient, we living animals are all alike a temporary brood of chaos. Our classic forms and our human arts are the flowers of one cosmic or planetary climate, scarcely attained before they are withered; and the knowledge of this predicament, in which life finds itself not by accident but just because it is life, because it is a movement from the forgotten into the unforeseen, first opens to us the door to the eternal and founds the ultimate religion of the spirit upon the very vanity of things.

HARMONY

HARMONY of impulses, perfect or imperfect, may exist on any scale; and poetic fancy often seems to discover it in wide ranges, such as the stellar universe or the universe of spirits, however quarrelsome and subject to collision and catastrophe these regions may be in reality. Certain landscapes, certain conjunctions of light and cloud, seem miracles of harmony to the eye; yet these conjunctions are accidental and evanescent, no vital trope being established there, to preserve or to reproduce them. The notion that any spirit lives in them would be superstitious; yet they may truly awaken organic harmonies in the eye of the painter or poet, with reverberations and affinities in the whole human psyche; and the resultant mood of the human spirit will be called the spirit of the scene.

So there are surely many harmonies in the depths of matter, partly traced in our chemistry; and it would be rash to affirm that in the formation of a resisting atom there was nothing akin to the spirit of an animal. Yet the scale and above all the

method of reproduction is so unlike that of our earthly
zoology, that the analogy may well be superficial. Perhaps the
secret of our sort of animation lies in the tendency of each organic unit to restore and to propagate itself; whereas the
formations we call inorganic, are not transmitted from one
individual to another, but generated in vast numbers, always
afresh, from a disparate fund of matter, like hailstones from a
cloud. The assimilation of all genesis in nature to animal
generation, so that like must produce like, has been one of
the chief sources of myth in philosophy. It has favoured the
groundless prejudice that mind could only arise from mind:
whereas mind, being something spiritual and unsubstantial, is
a finality or entelechy involved in motion, and incapable of
generating anything else. So, in another dimension, is any
phenomenon; yet when existence is reduced by superficial
analysis to a train of phenomena, so that all real genesis or
derivation must be denied, the notion that like ought to breed
like survives in the fancy, and phenomena are conceived
somewhat like swarms of summer flies, subject to habit, and
justifying their reappearance by the mere fact that they have
often appeared before. But habit and facility in repetition are
incongruous with pure essences, as Hume, the master of this
method, was quick to see: they reside rather in the human
psyche, which (though his phenomenalism forbade him to
say so) is a self-sustaining and developing organisation in
matter, like the life-cycle of insects, to which repetitions and
rhythms are congruous and native.

Most of the harmonies in nature would thus speak to spirit
by analogy only, by causing inner harmonies to vibrate in the

psyche, without signifying the existence of kindred spirits elsewhere, or establishing with them any spiritual communion. To support spiritual communion there must be physical affinity. Universal cosmic harmonies may be reduced to moonshine; because whilst a natural equilibrium, however unstable, cannot but subsist at every moment in the universe, this is as much an equilibrium of conflicts as of co-operation; and it is only distance that lends unity to the view. Evidently between any living creature and his habitat some degree of harmony must subsist, else that creature could never have been formed; and this indispensable radical harmony will not escape the spirit kindled at that centre: what indeed is this spirit but that very harmony raised to an actual unity, to a conscious motion and warmth and music coursing between the soul and the world? Such harmony must endure fundamentally so long as there is life; but it may be crossed and turned into agony by continual breaks in that harmony, portending disease, disaster, and death. Hence the pure notes of vision and pleasure rise only at rare moments above the dull tension of slumber and uneasiness; and as death in spots, no matter how frequent or epidemic, leaves the broad face of nature as placid as ever and her fecundity unimpaired, so the harmonies achieved in spots, in the life of specific organisms, leave nature free to disorganise or reorganise her immense domain as occasion may prompt, without mercy for the souls that perish, and without particular preference for those about to be born.

ULTIMATE RESPONSIBILITY

FEELINGS of anger, remorse, and vindictiveness are human: the desire to annihilate the foe, even to annihilate the past, cannot be removed. The folly of such a desire—since even the most hateful enemy might be *used*—leaves active the aggressive and destructive impulse, and therefore the murderous wish. At most, if both parties are capable of adaptation, they may agree to a sort of compromise in murder: this is the path of rational politics and morals. But natural hostility can never be really quenched; to extinguish it would be to extinguish the will to live. This is an argument for asceticism, when a delicate conscience recoils from eternal war and from a fundamental wilfulness in choosing a side. The ascetic solution does not exclude a sort of dying joy, very conspicuous in the cheerfulness of Buddhistic and Christian piety; love, justice, truth and death may be embraced together. After all even renunciation is a last act of will; and as people care prodigiously about their own funeral and grave, and the disposal of their other relics, so they fuss about peace. Life, while it lasts, must take some direction. Whatever buffets it from without or entangles it within must always seem as something evil, wrong, detestable, and to be extirpated as soon as possible. Every living thing, answering Hamlet's question beforehand, takes up arms against a sea of troubles, and by opposing attempts to end them; not with a capricious or wanton hostility but by virtue of a specific initial effort to exist and to continue.

Sometimes, however, the immediate object of vital wrath excuses itself, bows as it were apologetically, with a deprecatory smile, as if recognising the perfect natural justice of our anger. "It was not I," it seems to say, "it was my ancestors, my circumstances, my wicked partner. It was the devil in me." And if we credit this excuse, our hostility may pass over the head of the immediate offender, and may seek the true cause and source of his offending.

Alas! It is God.

That God is the great enemy, the taskmaster, the irresponsible thunderer, who launches the merciless stroke falling on us when we least expect it, was a common feeling among the ancients; but two circumstances conspired to disguise, without ever abolishing, this terrible essence of deity. One circumstance was the partial sympathy which this same deity evidently showed us; for good things as well as evil came from him abundantly; and so long as we live and prosper, or hope to do so, the good seems to prevail: and though the Lord be essentially the master, who may destroy us if he will, we may praise him because, in fact and so far, he has not destroyed us. The other circumstance is the partial sympathy which, even in his hostility, he awakens in us. Before we allow ourselves to be angry with him, we imagine that he is angry with us: and how much more magnificent, powerful, consecutive, and decisive is his wrath than ours! Hatred thus becomes awe, awe submission, and submission love: and the idea of deity takes on the form which modern religion has given it.

But where, now, is the object on which our vital resentment may light? When we stumble against a stone, we curse *it*; no doubt, on reflection, the stone cannot be much blamed: it is either the general cursedness of things (modified and mollified as above) or some dereliction in persons who have put the stumbling-block in our way, or finally some blindness or haste in ourselves. Ultimate guilt thus lodges either in God, i.e. in the nature of things, or in other persons, or in ourselves. But these two latter fountains of wickedness, though the more obvious and directly hateful, against whom invective is most commonly directed, are ultimately reducible to the first. For if we admit a voluntary creation and omnipresent providence, the acts of men, even of ourselves, are a part of the divine dispensation, our only ultimate friend or enemy. If we invest free-will and absolute beginnings with ultimate responsibility at many points in time and in many persons, the monotheism which I was assuming for convenience gives place to a metaphysical pluralism, in which God, if he is still introduced, is only *primus inter pares,* and has to live as best he may under a rain of inexplicable incidents and changes in the moral weather. The *conjunction* of just these persons, accidents, or wills becomes now the true fatality or nature of things; or the responsible deity to which praise and blame may ultimately attach.

[Continue this showing that diversity, if not meddlesome, is not hateful: so that only casual conjunctions, or the undirected economy, of nature, is to blame for anything.—*Santayana's own note at the end of this unfinished essay. D.C.*]

FRIENDSHIP

THE RELATION of love to friendship is a fascinating and enlightening subject never, as far as I know, properly treated. The ancients, who were masters in friendship, were tyros in love. Love for them was either like the rut and breeding of animals, unimaginative and without spiritual refinements; or else they turned it into a cosmic or divine influence in theory and into debauchery in practice. In order to humanise and ennoble this divine madness they introduced it into friendship, where it doesn't belong.

In modern times, the sentiment and the literature of love have been immensely developed and over-developed, but friendship has lost its ancient importance, and in its heroic forms has become obsolete. Yet I think that friendship has vital roots in human society as well worth watering as those of love. The seed of friendship is scattered by nature wherever cooperation extends beyond the family: it exists potentially when contemporaries begin spontaneously to help one another. Perhaps such cooperation among mammals first appears in war: I say among mammals, because cooperation among ants and bees, or unison in the flight of birds, baffles my powers of interpretation. But when two human males or (if this ever happens) two females fight on the same side, their action, if the principle of it were conscious, would involve friendship. Heraclitus said that war is the parent of all things; this could more properly be said of love; but his paradox seems to be confirmed in the case of friendship. It is in war, or in difficulties, that a man needs allies; if he finds them, he begins to conceive an *alter ego,* a part of nature that is not merely an object or a dark power, but is animated by a kindred soul.

But are there no kindred souls in the family? Is there no brotherly love? Certainly kittens crawl confidently over one another in the litter. Kittenish familiarity, however, is not friendship, but sheer disregard of others, except as cushions. The young despot is extending his absolute domination; he is coaxing and playful just as he is cruel, in the greedy luxury of his egoism. In brotherly love this egotism is corrected by the instincts, habits, and joint interests of the family. Children are drilled to do things together, and in the same way; their habits and sentiments become contagious; they will all cry or all laugh at once, hardly knowing why. A kind of gregarious sympathy or moral unison establishes itself unintentionally among them, against which later their individualities may rebel. We have here a family bond formed in the nest, entirely different from friendship, and often hostile to friendship. Friendship belongs to life in the open, when you have been fledged, and begun to explore the world for yourself and to discover your personal affinities. It is parallel to exogamy. It is the opposite of a stuffy brotherly or sisterly love, proper to the meek children in an orphanage that are all dressed alike, walk out two by two, hand in hand, and can hardly tell themselves apart.

Still, I confess that brotherly love can become distinct and discriminating, when it is an extension of paternal or filial feelings, and I have seen touching instances of it, especially between a big brother and a little one. The elder brother plays the papa; he has been charged with responsibility; he mustn't let his little brother be run over; he must lead him by the hand, or take him on his back, if the poor child grows too tired or sleepy. Here is a lesson in tenderness, and learnt all the more willingly, because after all it is a game. You are playing parent: it is almost as good as playing horse. And the little brother also, though he says nothing, is having a holiday. He is brisker than usual, transferring his trust from his mother to his big brother, someone nearer himself but still an authority: and this fresh and voluntary trust, this respect for an equal, is essentially friendship. Yet it is only a rehearsal: the brothers love each other without having chosen each other, they are not united by any non-family bond.

Friendship, then, is an essentially open air and public bond, that neither grows out of the home nor tends to establish a new home. It feeds on adventure and discovery: the emotion of it is a truant emotion, the emotion of living freely, boldly, even if not dangerously. But, again in contrast to brotherly love, it is distinctly selective, personal, and exclusive: in this respect it resembles the passion of love. They both excite the imagination, as brotherly love does not. But in friendship what excites the imagination is not the friendship itself, as in the case of falling in love, when the whole world becomes unimportant and an intruder, if only the love be returned. What fills the imagination of friends is the world, as a scene for action and an object of judgement; and the person of the friend is distinguished and selected from all others because of exceptionally acceptable ways of acting, thinking, and feeling about other things or other persons. Friendship is thus the union of two freely ranging souls that meet by chance, recognise and prize each other, but remain free.

When I speak of souls, I mean more than minds, and when I speak of union I mean more than agreement. Friendship, let me repeat, is something vital and biological. Minds may agree without knowing it or caring about it; persons may co-operate socially or economically without being united, as two nations may cooperate in continuing a war. The boys in the school in *Nicholas Nickleby* cooperated in keeping the school going, but they probably hated one another hardly less than they hated the school and the master. It is often so in politics, and that is what gives a moral and human dignity to the smallest ancient city or club founded on friendship, a dignity utterly absent in the modern State, or in the industrial system of any community. Here everything is based on accident, rivalry, competition, or on public necessities or private gain. There are sects, parties, and associations in plenty, but there is no friendship, because there is no spontaneous, motiveless selection of companions in life.

Even a spontaneous selection of the same life, as when two strangers join the same religious order, implies and produces no friendship; because there is no mutual selection of the persons that shall lead that life together. A fixed ulterior purpose congregates them, not a vital personal sympathy; each is pre-occupied with his secret problem; they may give each other a good example, or a certain gregarious support, as in singing hymns; but the persons are indifferent, transparent, and exchangeable. In friendship, as in love, the play must have the persons for its authors; it must not have been written beforehand for everybody to recite. The give and take in adventure and discovery, in laughter and in comment, becomes a sport freer and more prized than any ulterior object.

Friends may have contrasting characters or opinions, but imagination and sympathy in them must be able to bridge the chasm; they must feel the possibility of nursing that different opinion and having that different character for one's own. Friends thus seem to enact all those parts of oneself which fortune has suppressed. It follows that in a crisis, that calls for one's hidden resources, friends must find themselves acting together. If they take opposite sides then, their friendship turns out to have been an illusion. You may come upon *les frères ennemis,* you cannot come upon *les amis ennemis.* The same blood may flow into different beings that compete, but mutual understanding and trust are results that manifest a natural harmony. And I think that disappointments and alienations in love and friendship arise rather from false anticipations than from false perceptions and feelings. The instinctive sympathy has a true ground, but that ground is a living creature subject to change. If later and in other circumstances the soil that was fertile becomes sterile, if the stream that watered it has ceased to flow, that does not cancel the reality of the earlier flowers. The notion of swearing "eternal" love or friendship suffers from the equivocation latent in that word "eternal." If you understand it to mean everlasting, you are a fool. No fact, no feeling, can guarantee its own duration; much less feeling so highly conditioned, so precarious and accidental as the conjunction of two fluttering souls. Yet instinct, even here, is not deceived in its assurance, if by "eternal" is signified indelible; it is appealing, as love and friendship appeal when deep and clear, not to future time but to indelible truth. It is a modest, a spiritual, and a profound thing to say that this feeling or this faith can never change: of course when you are dead, or when that part of you is dead, the feeling will not continue to be felt by those other people or those other parts of yourself that may then survive. What you meant, if you had your wits about you, was that your soul and that feeling or faith were inseparable, that in that feeling or faith you had become yourself as never before, and once for all. Come then death if it will, it cannot destroy that *troth* in your faith and feeling. It cannot break your vow.

If in modern society friendship is starved for lack of [indecipherable], in ancient society it was variously denaturalised by fusion with less liberal interests. In love this fusion is normal, because love is a preface by nature, and ought to take root in the economy of life and morals and fulfil its secret function by creating a family and becoming the authority and benevolence of the old towards the young and the strong towards the weak. But when barbarians vowed friendship by tasting each other's blood, or when ancient philosophers said that friends should have all things in common, there was a materialisation of friendship involved. The spiritual vow of "eternal friendship," which expressed a union of souls, became a political contract, just as when love becomes marriage; and the community of sentiment and taste and free pleasures became a partnership or communism in worldly goods. Yet this communism, if it had ever been realised in fact, would have destroyed friendship and turned it into an odious obligation and a source of eternal enmity. It is essential to friendship to be free, and to assume no liability in matters below its liberal sphere. Naturally a friend will help a friend in need, as any Christian would help any man if he could: but that is an embarrassment and a danger to friendship. The benefitted man becomes a client, the benefactor becomes a patron. Such relations may be normal in certain cases, but they are not the proper relations between friends. As to having all things in common, that is only a rhetorical flourish. Wives, I suppose, were not to be common to the ideal friends; and while a true friend might adopt the children left by a dead companion, if they had no grandparents or uncle to take charge of them, that would be a special occasion for general benevolence, not a proof of true friendship between his lost friend and himself. It might be an incidental consequence of their friendship, if for instance, the survivor was already attached to his friend's children and they to him: but I am talking about the character of friendship as a sentiment, not about the effects that it may have incidentally in the world, which will differ in different phases of society.

Jealousy, masterfulness, the desire to monopolise are absent in friendship which has the essential quality of being a coincidence of free souls. Such coincidence can hardly extend to the whole soul, and never to the whole life. The parts of an organism cooperate and are inseparable; but that is not a case of friendship but of physical interdependence. One of the blessings of friendship is that it lifts us out of our physical commitments. From this it follows that all the material and involuntary part of our lives must be presupposed and must go on automatically before friendship arises; and that it would be an anomaly for friendship to interfere with that fundamental order. The question is not what effects friendship may have in the world, but what powers in the world may sustain or prevent friendship. Friendship is an elementary instance of something good in itself. The machinery that brings it about will have other developments, and will bring about other goods and evils; but we must not tax friendship itself with those consequences. It is something spiritual, a phase of freedom. It can have no consequences. One of the blunders of philosophy has been to think of freedom as a cause. Freedom is a result of perfect organisation. The problem is so to organise ourselves as to become free. Nature must do this for us, not a non-existent power called liberty; and our physical and psychical persons are the parts of nature that do this for the spirit within us, whenever they can.

If a man must be alert all day about his business, and grows drowsy in the evening over the habitual observations of his wife and his newspaper, friendship can hardly seem to him more than a memory of callow youth. He will have partners in business and colleagues in politics; and such co-operation might lead to friendship, if the colleagues or partners discovered that they sympathised strongly in some free and unofficial matter; but this is not likely. The unofficial matters (suppose they were sport or religion) would merely make them partners and colleagues together with other persons in those other affairs. The more they were interested in the thing the less they would be interested in the persons. Two shipwrecked men in a boat together are not likely to be in a free and convivial state of mind; they will discuss whether it would be better to row or to drift, to make for land or for a frequented sea-route, also in what direction these respectively lie, and they will probably not agree on these points. If they remain afloat long enough, it is likely that the thought will occur to each of them that the other is rather useless and tiresome, that he is consuming more than his share of the water and provisions, and that it would be a blessing if he fell overboard.

Forced adventures are no more favourable to friendship than are forced associations. Yet such is the character of what is called friendship between nations. It signifies that for the moment they are constrained to work together, because they fear and hate a third rival more than they hate or fear each other.

Philanthropy and a humanitarian conscience also exist, which may extend to all forms of life, but only when one's specific human standard is in abeyance. There exists also a specific spiritual life that in man at least may supervene upon his physical tendencies and powers; conscience is a part of this spiritual life; and when conscience is awakened in regard to the needs of strangers, enemies, the suffering or the poor, it is called charity. Humanitarianism is in part a derivative from Christian charity, when charity has ceased to be Christian and ascetic, and when the universal application proper to it has been assigned to some special standard of comfort or ethics. The humanitarian, like the missionary, is often an irreducible enemy of the people he thinks to befriend, because he has not imagination enough to sympathise with their proper needs nor humility enough to respect them as if they were his own. Arrogance, fanaticism, meddlesomeness, and imperialism may then masquerade as philanthropy.

Kindness, as the name implies, has its root in the family. The motherly heart cannot help, at moments, almost mistaking other children for her own; and the appeal of infants is felt by every human being, such kindness being originally perhaps a condition to the perpetuation of the race. This organic tenderness, when not too much taxed at home, can be applied to other objects. As the little girl cannot bear to neglect her doll, so the sentimentalist cannot bear to think of savages living so miserably, or the poor at home being so dirty, so ill-fed, and so ill-spoken. And the economic mind, which is the housekeeper's mind, cannot bear the disorder and waste of bad laws and of armed conflicts. A union of the motherly heart with the economic mind is admirable in the housewife, but it is ominous in the politician. He wants to redeem the poor, so that they may become more productive as

labourers and less revolutionary; he wants to civilise the
savages, so that they may create a new market for his home
manufactures and foreign trade. Thus while his countenance
radiates benevolence, his business and his missions ruin the
native civilisation and his philanthropy corrupts and exter-
minates the native race. He is the opposite of a friend to
mankind, for he aspires to turn them into raw material for
his own arts, and to standardise them after his own pattern,
so that the whole world may speak his language, think his
thoughts, and buy his merchandise. Mankind had no need of
any of these things, and has no love for them. But not being
their friend, he cares nothing for what they need or love, he
cannot even conceive it; and he prides himself on that in-
capacity as a superior virtue. That is why, in his benevolence,
he works night and day to help them to grow like himself or
to help them to disappear.

There is something of this aggressive egotism in militant
religions; an element that is not charity but corporate zeal.
Charity may also be present in the missionary; but this, as
the Catholic Church says, is a *supernatural* virtue: that is, it
transforms natural love into something spiritual. What do I
mean by "spiritual"? In this case I mean that charity, not
being intrinsic either to love or to friendship, requires the in-
tervention of imaginative reason, by which we detach ourselves from our accidental persons and circumstances and feel
the equal reality of all other persons in all other plights. Now
imaginative reason is the contrary of all that I was just now
attributing to the politician: it sympathises with all will, and
abets none. It launches or stimulates no enterprise, except pre-

cisely this habit of respecting them all, and of surrendering and denying in oneself whatsoever is contrary to the will in nature or, if you prefer, to the will of God. Charity therefore is a chastened and enlightened love. Though the labours of the philanthropist, when they are remedial, are charitable in effect, since they relieve distress without imposing new burdens, his constructive ambition is profoundly uncharitable. It overflows with gross illusions, and breeds new unnecessary conflicts, where charity would bring understanding and peace.

POLITICAL RELIGION

THE INTERPLAY of religion and politics is well illustrated in the fortunes of the Hebraic faith. What is distinctive of Judaism seems to have been originally only a religious sanction coming to justify a distinctly political wisdom or ambition; although purely poetic intuitions were not lacking, which had been current among the people from remote antiquity. Abraham and his tribe had lived in Ur of the Chaldees, near the Persian gulf, and had been pagans and worshippers of the moon. But "now the Lord had said unto Abraham, Get thee out of thy country and from thy kindred, and from thy father's house, unto a land that I will show thee. And I will make of thee a great nation, and will bless thee, and make thy name great; and thou shalt be a blessing. And I will bless them that bless thee, and curse them that curseth thee; and in thee shall all families of the earth be blessed." *

The militant spirit of this new tribal unity and of this

* Genesis, XII, 1–3.

prophecy of universal dominion did not altogether erase the magic of that full moon shining over the desert, which had so long spoken to the heart of nomads and herdsmen, and given them a measure for their seasons. Even when all impersonation of the moon as a goddess or a god had been eclipsed by a more human and political deity, the sacredness of a celestial meter clung to the calendar and lent a peculiar fixity to those sabbaths, economically so convenient, which marked her quarters.

The native facility with which a religious experience comes to express and to sanction a political hope appears, with wonderful force and frankness, in the vow of Jacob:

And Jacob went out from Beer-sheba, and went toward Haran. And he lighted upon a certain place, and tarried there all night, because the sun was set; and he took of the stones of that place, and put them for his pillows, and lay down in that place to sleep. And he dreamed, and behold a ladder set up on the earth, and the top of it reached to heaven: and behold the angels of God ascending and descending on it. And, behold, the Lord stood above it, and said, I am the Lord God of Abraham thy father, and the God of Isaac: the land whereon thou liest, to thee will I give it, and to thy seed; and thy seed shall be as the dust of the earth, and thou shalt spread abroad, to the west and to the east, and to the north, and to the south: and in thee and thy seed shall all the families of the earth be blessed. And, behold; I am with thee, and will keep thee in all places wither thou goest, and will bring thee again into this land: for I will not leave thee, until I have done that which I have spoken to thee of.

And Jacob awakened out of his sleep and he said: Surely the Lord is in this place, and I knew it not. And he was afraid, and said, How dreadful is this place! this is none other but the house of God, and this is the gate of heaven. And Jacob rose up early in the morning, and took the stone that he had put for his pillows, and set it up for a pillar, and poured oil upon the top of it. And he called the name of that place Beth-el; but the name of that city was called Luz at the first. And Jacob vowed a vow, saying, If God will be with me, and will keep me in this way that I go, and will give me bread to eat, and raiment to put on, so that I come again to my father's house in peace; then shall the Lord be my God; and this stone, which I have set for a pillar, shall be God's house: and of all that thou shalt give me, I will surely give the tenth unto thee.

We could not ask for a fairer instance than this of political religion; for if the political motive and calculation in it are unblushing, the faith as well as the imagery are genuinely religious. Feigning or fostering religion for a political purpose, as politicians sometimes do or are accused of doing, would not be to render religion political: it would be to employ other people's religious customs or interests, by a profane ruse, in a purely political or social calculation. But in Jacob religious imagination and religious faith are congenital. That they play into the hands of his political ambition only redoubles his allegiance to them, in all their supernatural revelations. He does not in the least suspect that it was political ambition and commercial militancy that secretly inspired his dream, and that perhaps less secretly inspired his father to send him on this pious journey, that he might choose a wife from his own people, and not a daughter of the Canaanites, whose country they had invaded. The wise Isaac knew that mixed marriages were dangerous to the cohesion of the tribe and to the individuality of their religion. Religious zeal and political courage were doubtless fused inextricably in his mind. And the dread, the awe, that fill Jacob's own mind upon waking are purely religious. He is sure that he has found the place where earth may communicate with heaven, and that the Lord, the power that rules nature and fortune, has spoken to him, and renewed the promises made to Abraham, his grandfather. What a providential encouragement in his life-work! And he will not let the occasion slip. He will mark and consecrate the spot, lest the Lord should forget it; and he will make a vow, and keep it, if God continues to protect him, to offer on this altar, which he now proclaims to be the Lord's house, one tenth of the produce of his flocks and of the booty of his wars.

Religion and politics may thus come into the world together, like twins; and it is not unlikely that religion may have been the first-born. That ladder to heaven with those angels ascending and descending are evident gifts of *la fonction fabulatrice*. They do not bring earthly gifts or promises; they mark a path for wayfarers into a calmer and clearer world. And the subsequent development of Judaism and of its offshoots proves that this visionary and ideal element could easily reassert itself and either supersede the political element altogether or at least subordinate and somewhat refine it.

There is a peculiarity in the Jewish view, as revealed by this early witness, that may be worth noting. Religious faith and religious imagery subsist to the end, but reflection does not elaborate them; they remain inarticulate. It is the political interest, the militant element, that reason gradually elaborates;

so that in the end the effects of religion in the lay world, its moral and social utility, become its rational sanction, and whatever faith is allowed to subsist turns into animal faith, the spontaneous assumption that life is worth living, the world worth enjoying, and the science of it the only knowledge and the only ideality that rewards itself. When this conclusion is reached, which is not often, we have a purely political religion: a religion still, because it continues to proclaim a particular religious system as the providential source of social welfare: yet this appeal to religious instrumentalities does not in any way consecrate either public institutions or individual lives to a spiritual ideal. The ultimate and all-inclusive good remains political. The tenth that policy may offer to heaven is like that vowed by Jacob: a prudent insurance, to secure the safer enjoyment of the other nine tenths.

According to this use of words I should not call Catholicism or Islam political religions. They are *religious* religions. When in power they become theocracies. Far from submerging their religious message in utility for profane life, they constrain lay life, if they can, to serve as a pedestal and occasion for the triumph of spirit. That this is the case with the Catholic Church, I will not stop to argue at length. The matter is complicated because the "Kingdom of Heaven" is a second promised land, towards which mankind is summoned to march under pain of hell fire; and the narrow path leading there is prescribed by divine authority. This is therefore a theocratic system in essence and political only in that sense. Yet this Kingdom of Heaven is supernatural: it can be established on earth only on the destruction of "this world"; and it can be established in the heart (for it is an ambiguous dispensation) only by a radical reversal and sacrifice of the will. The political regimen imposed is therefore only a means to a non-political end; and such a religion, just because it operates politically with non-political aims is odious to the politician, and tolerable to the man of the world only because he does not find it disagreeable as a convention and never dreams of taking it seriously as a philosophy.

The most brilliant example of a militant reforming religion is Islam; and being simpler than Christianity, it shows better how a system that involves conquest and a revealed law, absorbing politics into its universal mission, is not a political religion in the sense of reducing religion to an instrument of secular government. What inspired Mohammed? Surely not the love of wealth or conquest for their own sake. He was a peaceful merchant for years; and amid the burning deserts and under the intense skies of Arabia, where profound meditation and lyric eloquence are natural to everybody, he had ample leisure to think, and enough contacts with the world to know and detest superstitions that prevailed in it. But it was not to destroy traditional religion that his zeal was moved, but only to purify it. Among the popular cults at Mecca was that of the Kaaba, which he retained; and he revered and envied the Jewish and Christian treasure of sacred books. Why should not the Arabs possess one as well? Commercial and erotic thoughts also occupied him, and he saw no cause to banish them: but all must be received and retained as the gift of Allah, the immediate, pervasive, all-seeing, all-working will of God. It was this intense presence

of the Unfathomable that inspired him and imposed on him
the vocation of a prophet and of a conqueror. Away, then,
with all vain dogma and ritual. Let religion become a perpetual direct prayer, an uninterrupted colloquy with God.
What secrets, what music, what rapture might not break in
upon that sacred solitude? What wise monitions also for the
conduct of life? To what submission, to what courage, to
what sublime identification with divine power might not the
spirit, so fortified, attain? The revelation that broke in upon
Mohammed was as religiously immediate as it was politically
wise. In a recurrent trance he heard the angel of God dictate
to him the words of the Koran: words, he was sure, eternally
audible in the mind of Allah, and learned there by his faith-
ful messenger. The words are many and in various keys,
lyrical, prophetic, didactic, biographical; but the magic of
those words lies rather in the Voice that utters them. The ob-
viousness of monotheism shines like the full moon over the
desert and with an equal clearness faith floods the heart of
the believer, at once humble, free, and aristocratic in its absolute militancy. He can play the prince and the beggar by
turns with an equal dignity. He will disdain drink, because it
fuddles, and will assert lust, because there his virility is tri-
umphant. Towards unbelievers his domination will not be
fussy or meddlesome or ordinarily covetous: let them continue to eat all the filth they like; but he will keep his superiority silent and unsullied; by antecedent submission and
constant recollection of the will of Allah, he has embraced his
whole destiny and concentrated his whole soul without compromise or fear.

We must not be misled if we hear that the armies of Islam are brave because those ruffians are persuaded that if they die in battle, in the Paradise of the Prophet they may at once begin to enjoy an endless succession of copulations refreshed by an endless succession of sherbets. These are popular symbols for violent will and delicate pleasure; but delicate pleasure and violent will have other manifestations. The point is to accept and enact one's part in the predestined play: for that is pure life, cleared of all servitude and of all nonsense. The mystic is here not out of key with the sensualist or the despot; each, in Moslem society, understands and allows the others. The system, when dominant, is a theocracy, like Judaism and Christianity, though franker. It does not condemn or disregard material goods; its summary cosmology absolutely reduces fortune to fate; but its no less summary virtue by no means subordinates spirit to matter. On the contrary, it is spirit that invincibly dominates here over both matter and fate, by taking all they offer and asking for nothing they refuse. Allah has apportioned these things for us. How should we, in whom the mind of Allah is reflected, be such cowards as not to endure his laws or not to enjoy his gifts?

Political religion, as I use the term, always preserves a spiritual factor, else it would have lapsed into political hypocrisy; and this spiritual factor may at any time reassert its supremacy and protest that it is in itself the greatest of human goods and not to be judged by the incidental services that it may render to the state. So for instance the Church of England (founded in the very act of proclaiming the dependence of religion on politics and declaring the King, who was a despotic layman, the head of the national Church) has always contained a party that privately clung to its divine authority and independence: a party that in the nineteenth century publicly undertook to restore its original doctrine and ritual, to reconvert England to orthodox Christianity, and to become in fact what it liked to call itself, a branch of the Catholic Church.

The love of absolutism, ingrained in all governments, was far from being the only interest that made the Church of England a part of the State; the same worldliness and prepotency that ruled the King were evidently prevalent also among the clergy, else the change of allegiance could hardly have taken place; and indeed we may say, from the religious point of view, that nothing better demonstrates the real corruption that had infected the Catholic Church than the character of the Reformation itself, the shocking personalities of its leaders, the worldliness of their passions, and the fundamental blindness of their theologies. And yet, when once these monsters had established their various forms of religion, the people who were told that their religion had not been changed, but only purified, and were given the Bible to read for themselves, did not cease, when the spirit was in them, to draw from it for themselves, under the spell of obscure phrases and hallowed precepts, various types of sincere devotion.

The Bible is a wonderful source of inspiration for those who do not understand it. Yet in the end the influence of lay life and national wars kept these elements of veritable religion subject to secular control. Among the Calvinists it was rather trade that profited by righteousness and sanctioned it; among the Lutherans rather devotion to the State, relieved religiously by a warm sense of safety in reliance on the unmerited grace of God. The supports of the Church of England, which was more ecclesiastical, were more aristocratic. It had been the new nobility under Henry VIII and Elizabeth that had gathered the spoils of the Church, especially of the monasteries: and after 1688 the landed upper class was well pleased to protect the rural clergy and to give the right national tone to the bishops. They wished above all things to preserve a certain proud manliness of character and insularity of mind, together with lordliness of position: the whole sanctioned at emotional crises, according to precedents in the Old Testament, by a wave of national religious pride and religious assurance. What I understand by political religion could not be better exemplified. It is genuinely religious, but the occasions that stir the heart and the hopes that it nurses are not only earthly but intensely political.

The ancient Jews themselves, political and national as was the triumph they looked to, always coloured their faith with reliance on miracles; and they even developed a deeper spiritual allegiance in certain circles that made that triumph seem rather a moral and mystical transformation of their own hearts; and this interpretation became orthodox, without excluding political hopes, when the Prophets and the Psalms were added to the Law. The ritual duties imposed by the latter were not abandoned, but the language of them could be understood mystically; a spiritual motive for keeping the

Law might be found in the love of it, and of the beauty of
the Lord's house. Peace and holiness might be preferred to
glory and domination, and the forces of the State might be
conceived only as a bodyguard for the Temple. Political religion would then have digested its own flesh and proclaimed
the supremacy of spirit. This might have happened in Britain
if its vital centres had not been London or Edinburgh, but
Oxford or Canterbury; and if its rivers had not been the
Thames, the Tyne, the Mersey, and the Clyde, debouching
into broad estuaries and navigable seas, but some fordable
Jordan feeding a dead lake amid the dead mountains of
Tibet or of Judaea.

Philosophically such a transformation would not be complete unless the natural rewards of piety were discarded altogether, and a material resurrection and a material heaven
were explained away as metaphors. So drastic a reform, however, would be contrary to Jewish and Catholic orthodoxy.
These religions, even when interpreted most spiritually, must
retain a political character. Not only, for instance, must Christ
be proclaimed to be already rightfully King over this world,
but the gratification of many earthly affections is promised in
the world to come. The philosopher or the mystic may be allowed to think reason or love its own reward; but only if
they do not turn away from all the unnecessary sweets that
are officially provided for the saints in addition.

ON PUBLIC OPINION

PUBLIC OPINION is like the wind; it becomes at times a formidable force, something a man finds himself borne along by or fighting against; yet in itself it is invisible, rises suddenly in gusts and squalls, and mysteriously disappears. If we ask ourselves what it is, we may perceive that the phrase, "public opinion," is characteristically fabulous, after the manner of literary philosophy: for the public is not a living organism, with senses and an intellect that can form opinions about ulterior matters. What is meant is some once private opinion that has turned into a form of words now prevalent among the public. Yet more than that is implied. For there are a thousand verbal opinions habitually prevalent in society, for instance about the weather or about money, that are not classed under public opinion, because each man feels them to spring up spontaneously in himself, by the suasion of his senses or most secret impulses: and the fact that other people feel as he does seems to him not a matter of public opinion but a consequence of human uniformity, like having two legs.

Thus "public opinion" does not signify merely private opinions prevalent amongst the public, but such opinions when they touch matters in public dispute or are due to contagion, having not been formed spontaneously among the people but imposed on them by eloquence or iteration. They are parrot opinions. Yet it is by contagion that mankind is most easily, radically, and perfectly educated. By contagion we learn our mother tongue and develop our deepest sentiments. This contagion of example is the greatest of blessings when that example is good: that is to say, when in following it we develop our powers without subjecting ourselves to any alien domination.

Public opinion may therefore be prevalent and even intolerant without being tyrannical, if it merely anticipates, as in rational precepts and true information, that which each individual would have at last discovered painfully for himself. In sparing him that labour and saving him from following false scents, this education liberates his energies, if he has them, to advance independently beyond public opinion, along the same chosen paths; and if he lacks energy, this same education at least domesticates him happily in his proper spiritual home. How far unanimity in a given community may be natural and how far artificial is a biological question to be answered in each case separately, according to the circumstances; but we may safely say that unanimity can never be absolute. The universal shout represents a thousand different sentiments, and outrages many a silent heart; and even when the wave of passion buries all private differences, as it often does for a moment, when the wave subsides the differences come again to the surface, and that unanimity begins to seem, in retrospect, an ignominious drunken unanimity. The leaders, to whom the sentiment then dominant may have been natural and ineradicable, will then be driven to propaganda, or to perpetual preaching in special circles; while the indifferent crowd goes about its private affairs with a smile or a sneer, or a conventional affectation of deference. Then, even if the expression of public opinion seems to be unanimous, in religion, morals, or politics, it will not be unanimous really. It may even not exist at all, if the current expression of it signifies nothing but a cynical or prudent conformity to custom, for the sake of convenience or of ulterior interests. In a complex society, in which various traditions have been superposed and subsist together, there is sometimes a curious coexistence of two contrary public opinions on the same subject, as there used to be about duelling. Everybody as a Christian condemned the practice and everybody as a man of honour approved of it and conformed to it. I think much the same thing happens in regard to immortality. All modern religions—and almost everybody accepts some form of religion—assert it: yet everybody in his secular life and in making his will ignores it, and would be surprised and annoyed to hear it spoken of, out of church, as if it were a fact.

I think, however, that variability is less useful and amiable in public opinion than in the private mind. The private mind begins without experience, quite properly asks every sort of question, and is capable when mature of original ideas and discoveries. But public opinion moves without memory or possible method on a background of antideluvian prejudices: its immediate organs are custom, hearsay, and eloquence, three things not conducive to progress. Yet custom, though conservative and in itself irrational, normally has some *raison d'être:* at least it cannot be so absurd as to have proved suicidal. And many customs rest on primary instincts and social necessities, as language and conscience do; so that the public opinion that insists on them is right in being conservative. It is far more likely to be wise than is any reversal of it. Eloquence, also, though it intoxicates, draws its power from radical impulses and latent aspirations in human nature which it stirs up and brings suddenly to the surface. It may inspire the maddest action, yet it does *inspire:* and this awakening of the soul, however inopportune, opens up a vista towards some real good that wisdom should take account of. It is only the domination of hearsay, vulgar irresponsible hearsay, without piety or eloquence, that renders public opinion helpless and dangerous, inconstant without originality, and destructive without understanding what it destroys. The merciless oblivion that falls then upon things foreign or past removes all possibility of wisdom in political action.

The ballast of wisdom that public opinion draws in a primitive society from custom and eloquence, it draws in a highly organised society from institutions. Institutions are incorporated customs, customs sanctioned by express enactment, or prescribed and perpetuated by special classes of men, like priests, magistrates, or physicians. To keep lunar feasts and divide the month into quarters or weeks, giving each day of the week the name of some planet, was an ancient custom with some peoples; but the Hebrew Sabbath was an institution. So to sing occasionally is a habit, perhaps older than articulate speech; but it becomes an institution when choirs are trained to sing particular hymns on particular days. Spontaneous virtue here turns before our eyes into traditional domination. Institutions define and impose certain customs, which seem to lose the plasticity of nature; on the other hand, they accumulate experience, and supply an enduring basis for elaboration and refinements in the chosen art. At every stage an institution, since it builds on the achievements of its past, carries on a greater body of experience; and it thereby really increases the number of points from which further variations may start. Yet such happy development in the arts cannot be long continued, because human nature retains potentialities neglected by the original choice of a method and a particular direction of growth; and the inspired man cannot be content to go on forever refining the old method and expanding the old theme. He prefers to break away altogether, and begin again at the beginning in a new direction.

Public opinion, too, starts perpetually at the beginning, because all the potentialities of human nature stir unrecognised somewhere in the midst of a crowd; and almost any suggestion will find a response somewhere, at least for a moment. But almost all such awakenings die down at once, like a fire in straw. There is nothing at hand to feed or support them, and the mind lets them drop a little sadly, but resignedly, taking refuge in its old commonplaces and its old vices.

Sometimes, however, the new suggestion proves opportune, the spark becomes a bonfire, and there is an attempt at a real revolution, or a seeming success in it. I say a *seeming* success, because it would be a miracle if a popular cry, founded on no knowledge and representing no broad or constant force in human society, should really initiate a fresh set of institutions. It may at best establish a new nomenclature (as the French and Russian revolutions did for a time) and put in office a new set of men, who will repeat the biography of all governments, if they succeed in retaining power after they have ceased to destroy and begin to construct.

The real change, the radical revolution, will not have been the work of public opinion or of human intention at all. Revolutions do not succeed, they are not even attempted, in healthy commonwealths. Your successful revolutionaries are like malicious doctors at a death bed, who should boast of having killed the patient. They may have wished to do it, and he may have died. They may even have made a fatal injection at the moment when he was about to expire. But he would have died without their help; for if he had been curable they never would have been called to his bedside, nor nursed those hostile intentions. The reformers are themselves symptoms of the public disease.

Health is not conscious of itself, but frees the mind for the perception of other things; and even the joy of health, when it comes to the surface, comes rather in the form of some generous enthusiasm for nature, for sport, or for loveable people. So the health of society does not express itself in public opinion but in public affections, in a general enhanced vitality in all the arts, without controversial theories about them. But when society is deeply troubled, when men do not know what to do, what to think, what to enjoy, or how to avoid hateful compulsions, then every complaint and every panacea gathers adherents, parties arise, and ideologies fill the atmosphere with their quarrels. The misfortunes that meantime overtake the public are attributed to the party lately in power, but they continue unabated; so that the alternation of parties is rapid, yet less disastrous than a naive observer might have suspected. For beneath the follies that each successive party may advocate or even carry out, the vital constitution of society, with its traditional customs and pleasures, continues undisturbed; strangely undisturbed on the whole even amid the most cruel wars. Therefore each party can "point with pride" at the degree of prosperity or at the public works that graced its administration; for all these ideologies are too superficial and these men too commonplace to make much difference in the natural course of events, upward or downward, as the circumstances of the age may determine. For there are real revolutions in things, migrations, and confusion of peoples, decay and invention in the arts, intensification or disappearance of commerce: and on such real mutations the ideas and the shouts of the public play a thin and inconstant treble.

ALTERNATIVES TO LIBERALISM

WHY be troubled if events do not everywhere follow the liberal programme of progress? This programme is a party document, demanding the success of liberalism—apparently its ultimate and eternal success. But liberalism presupposes very special conditions. It presupposes a traditional order from which the world is to be emancipated. It presupposes heroic reformers, defying that order, and armed with a complete innate morality and science of their own by which a new order is to be established. But when once the traditional

As Santayana had been living in Rome for some years, the editor of the *Saturday Review of Literature*—Henry Seidel Canby—had written asking him for an essay on Fascism. This kind of a request rather irritated Santayana: he was not especially interested in a local regimen in Italy, but in the wider political questions that he later treated in his book on *Dominations and Powers*. As he wrote me in a letter on April 4, 1934: "It will not be on Fascism strictly but on *Order*." The essay "Alternatives to Liberalism" was published on June 23 of the same year as the leading article in Canby's review.

order has been thoroughly destroyed, that kind of heroic reformer may well become obsolete. His children will have no
grievances and perhaps no morality. Even the abundance of
their independent sciences, without an ultimate authority to
synthesize or interpret them, may become a source of bewil-
derment. Nothing may remain except a mechanical hurly-
burly, moral disintegration, and intellectual chaos. Add inter-
necine war and a break-down in industry, and there may
seem to be occasion for turning over a new leaf. As to what
may be found, or may come to be written, on the next page
no political programme can give us any assurance. Under
different circumstances in various places different new things
may appear, or various old things under different names.

The word liberalism sometimes describes a method of government and sometimes a principle of thought. If liberalism
were simply a principle of thought it would throw the mind
open to all alternatives. It would smile on all types of society,
as on the birds, reptiles, and carnivora at the zoo. It would
remember that every organic being prizes its own type of perfection and strives to preserve and to reproduce it. In so far,
however, as liberalism is a method of government, it may
well cause those who live under it to think any other method
of government strange and irrational, or even wicked; especially well-to-do people, since liberalism protects their comfort
and otherwise lets them alone. Even more vexatious systems,
when established by law and custom, come to seem like one's
native language, alone normal and intelligible. In this way
liberalism as a method of government may end by making
liberalism difficult as a method of thought. Hence the sur-

prise and distress of so many liberals at the appearance of a
Lenin, a Mussolini, or a Hitler.

I think that liberalism in thought—in other words, impartial philosophy—is equally possible under all forms of society,
because it is never social. It eludes social pressure. A man
anywhere may find an intellectual satisfaction in seeing things
through their causes and not through current passions, and
may learn sympathetically to appreciate their intrinsic merits.
Disinterested insight is permitted to any fish in any river,
provided he can get his nose out of the water.

But no, say our immersed philosophers, you can't live out
of your native element. You can't breathe mere air; and
where there is no life there can be no sympathy or intelligence. You must see things, they tell us, through your warm
passions, or everything will seem ghostly. However much you
may air yourself and try to be impersonal and speculative,
you will still be looking at the world from your watery home,
and with your fishy eyes; but you may have lost your vital
impetus and love of swimming. Better, then, keep your head
busily under water, and follow your bait.

This gospel of total immersion would appear to confirm
the liberal mind in its autonomy; yet this very absoluteness in
the individual, this perfect satisfaction in his own impulses
and opinions, since it is attributable also to others, drives him
to an ulterior impartiality and liberalism of thought. His constitutional confinement to his own person and circumstances
becomes a humourous predicament in his own eyes, and his
true spirit escapes into an international and superhuman liberty. Indeed, I think the best inspiration of liberalism has

been the desire to lift all men, as far as possible, into such enlightenment. For that purpose barriers were to be broken
down, and poverty and prejudice cleared away. The forms
which the free mind might take, since it was free, could not
be predetermined; and the sphere of government was accordingly limited to the protection of life and property. But in
practice that ulterior free life, in religion, art, and polite letters, remained rather confused and vaporous: those were after
all fantastic matters of merely private concern. It might almost be said that only material interests, closely guarded by
law, were felt to be important; and that the free life beyond,
the supposed justification of everything, was moonshine.

This result would have been more obvious, were there not
certain intermediate fields, like education, national defense,
and inheritance, to which liberal principles have never been
thoroughly applied. If, for instance, the state undertakes education and makes it compulsory, it has refused in that respect
to be a liberal state and has become paternal. The matter was
too important to be left to chance; it was too important to be
left to miscellaneous religious bodies. Yet the same solicitude
and the same constructive impulse would consistently justify
the state in controlling industry, sport, amusements, art, and
religion. Then government would have assumed the total
control of life in the governed, and the liberal division of
functions between material order and moral liberty would
have been abandoned.

Totally to control life in the governed and render society
organic has always been the aim of theocracies, and was the
ideal proposed on rational moral grounds by Plato and

Hegel. This ideal was actually realized in ancient city-states, as far as the slipshod character of human existence permitted. But such an ideal is incompatible with Christianity, which reserves the things that are God's, to form a revealed, international, spiritual system from which nevertheless many moral and practical consequences flow, affecting the things that are Caesar's. A modern social autocracy would have to choose, and either declare itself officially Christian, accepting those supernatural presuppositions as part of its structure, or else extirpate Christianity altogether, as the Roman Empire, Islam, and the French Revolution felt a strong impulse to do, though the event eluded them. Italy seems to have chosen the first alternative, and Russia the second, while Germany hesitates, torn between the glory of being wholly heathen and the fact of being partly Christian.

The dream of unanimity is glorious because human nature is social even in its freest flights, longing for approval, for moral support, for sweeping enthusiasms. There is therefore some difficulty in carrying out the liberal project, apparently so simple, of regulating only material things legally, while leaving spiritual things to private initiative. Such private initiative at once takes to propaganda. Having eluded social pressure, we proceed to exert it. Even philosophers and literary critics seem to be deeply unhappy if other literary critics and philosophers do not agree with them. Now if individuals and sects feel compelled to proselytize, might it not be simpler and more decent that the work of propaganda should be committed by the government to persons educated in their subjects, and probably saner and more in sympathy with the national temperament than a lot of discordant agitators would be likely to be? Certainly official minds are not fountains of originality. The virtues and truths to be disseminated must have taken shape spontaneously in individuals, perhaps in foreigners; but it remains for the genius of the age and nation to adopt and adapt these gifts according to its necessities. It has been governments, for the most mixed motives, that have usually taken the decisive step in religious and moral transformations, such as the establishment of Christianity, the Reformation, and the liberal revolution itself. These novelties were imposed by decree, after some change of monarch or court intrigue or military victory, on whole populations innocent of the business. So today it is remarkable how swiftly a virtual unanimity can be secured in a great and well-educated nation by the judicious management of public ceremonies, of the press and the radio. Perhaps without official coercion it would be impossible to form a definite type of citizen in our vast amorphous populations, and to create an unquestioning respect for a definite set of virtues and satisfactions. And perhaps mankind, without such moral unanimity, might find little glory or joy in living. It would be by no means necessary to suppress freedom of thought. To those who know their own will no knowledge is dangerous; it all becomes useful or pleasant. No serious book need be prohibited; and the publication of anything whatsoever might be allowed, if the form was suitable for specialists and the price high enough. But there should be no unauthorized propaganda, and no diffusion of cheap lies.

Above all, no lies inserted in the state catechism. The whole force of authority lies in speaking for realities, for necessities interwoven before man was man into the very texture of things. This is not to demand that any official philosophy, or even the human senses or reason, should be clairvoyant or omniscient: such a demand would be preposterous. All that is needed or possible is that the myths and slogans approved by authority should express pertinently the real conditions of human life, harmonizing action and emotion with the sides of reality important for human happiness. Here I seem to see a grave danger threatening the restorations of organic society that are being attempted in our day. Our minds are sophisticated, distracted, enveloped in a cloud of theories and passions that hide from us the simple fundamental realities visible to the ancients. The ancients were reverent. They knew their frailty and that of all their works. They feared not only the obvious powers bringing flood, pestilence, or war, but also those subtler furies that trouble the mind and utter mysterious oracles. With scrupulous ceremony they set a watchtower and granary and tiny temple on some gray rock above their ploughed fields and riverside pastures. The closed circle of their national economy, rustic and military, was always visible to the eye. From that little stronghold they might some day govern the world; but it would be with knowledge of themselves and of the world they governed, and they might gladly accept more laws than they imposed. They would think on the human scale, loving the beauty of the individual. If their ordinances were sometimes severe under stress of necessity, that severity would be rational, or at least amenable to reason. In such a case, holding truth by the hand, authority might become gentle and even holy.

Now, on the contrary, we sometimes see the legislator posing as a Titan. Perhaps he has got wind of a proud philosophy that makes the will absolute in a nation or in mankind, recognizing no divine hindrance in circumstances or in the private recesses of the heart. Destiny is expected to march according to plan. No science, virtue, or religion is admitted beyond the prescriptions of the state. Every natural whim is sacred, every national ambition legitimate. Here is certainly an intoxicating adventure; but I am afraid a city so founded, if it could stand, would turn out to be the iron City of Dis. These heroes would have entrenched themselves in hell, in scorn of their own nature; and they would have reason to pine for the liberal chaos from which their Satanic system had saved them. Fortunately on earth nothing lasts for ever; yet a continual revulsion from tyranny to anarchy, and back again, is a disheartening process. It obliterates the sane traditions that might have prevented this see-saw if they had been firmer and more enlightened.

TOM SAWYER AND DON QUIXOTE

SOME MONTHS ago, when I confessed that I had never read any of Mark Twain's principal books but knew only *The Jumping Frog* and other "funny stories" drawn from his writings, Mr. Cyril Clemens * kindly sent me a copy of Huckleberry Finn for my better enlightenment. And I had not read far in that book when a vague sense came over me that the ghost of Don Quixote stalked in the background. This feeling took definite shape when Tom Sawyer entered the scene and took the lead in planning the rescue of the old fugitive slave that Huck was concealing; for this was a difficult, dangerous, secret adventure freely undertaken at the call of Tom's native courage and the cry of the oppressed—a mission undertaken, too, without the ordinary selfish interest, since the victim was no lovely princess ready to fall into her

* The editor of the *Mark Twain Quarterly,* and a relation of the famous American writer. This essay appeared in that journal (Winter 1952).

rescuer's arms, but an old Negro trying to escape captivity. There had been the same disinterestedness in Don Quixote and the same romantic lead of the imagination, overruling legality and convention, as well as common sense, in the name of the inner man, heroically autonomous.

This, in Mark Twain's young heroes, is chiefly boyish play and love of mischief; yet in the case of Tom Sawyer it goes with a curious respect for superstitious prescriptions and ceremonies, often involving vigils and labours of the most exacting kind, with pain and wounds cheerfully accepted. All this, at least in the romances that had turned Don Quixote's head, contained a mixture of belief in witchcraft and magic, with something of Christian penance and martyrdom. This mixture was essential to chivalry which united the principle of honour, essentially the voice of the inner man, romantic, personal, and independent, with the principle of charity, bound to relieve all suffering, and to protect innocence against corruption. Now, Don Quixote, who was mad, could confuse this Christian charity with honour, and could sally forth on his own authority to right wrongs everywhere. When, at the end of his history, Cervantes represents his hero to have recovered his sanity, and to have confessed the folly of his imaginary knight-errantry, the dying man retains all his dignity; for his sanity washes away, so to speak, only the mud from his armour, only the ridiculous claims from his generous aspirations. The Christian order, which he now recognises to be alone authoritative, is, after all, itself, like romantic heroism, an imagined fulfilment of the inner man's demands. In banishing casual or fantastic loves, it retains love pure and all-embracing, and in denying victories to ambition it promises them to fidelity.

How would this matter stand with Mark Twain's two boys? When they grew up and dropped the remnants of their childish respect for hearsay and magic, what would absorb their moral allegiance? Would it be another supernatural world, enveloping this one and righting all its wrongs? Without my pointing to the Missouri of today to answer this question for me, I think there are cues enough in the author's text to suggest what the answer should be.

When the young Huck, for instance, considers that he may go to hell if he breaks the law by abetting the old slave's flight, he manfully decides to save him and to damn his own soul, if necessary. This is characteristically simple and decisive. In the case of Tom the issue would ultimately be the same: namely, the supremacy of affection over law and convention and that of personal will over any calculus of effects. Yet Tom Sawyer is more complex, more imaginative, and bolder than his poorer, less educated, and tenderer friend. There is a circumstance about his most elaborate and perilous adventure that shows us what it is that means most to him. Huck's whole heart was set on letting his devoted friend escape from the hut where he was then in hiding. Tom immediately takes the case in hand and devises all the details that must be set "right," according to the rules of romantic fiction, to give the proper dignity to the prison and prepare the proper means of escape. The conspiracy becomes a vast undertaking; underground passages and secret doors must be made, long fasts and long watches kept, and the right astrological moment waited for to effect the midnight flight. Huck and his unfortunate prisoner endure all this nonsense meekly and finally get away, hotly pursued. Tom himself, who serves as a rearguard, is wounded and caught by the pursuers. Then it appears that he knew from the beginning that the fugitive slave was no longer a slave at all. His mistress had died, leaving him a free man in her Will. For Tom it had all been private theatricals, done to the life by the other deluded actors, and by his own irresistible love of make-believe. For Tom Sawyer, young as he was, was not mad like Don Quixote. He was aware of the futility of his stage setting, and the serious trouble it caused. But everything, he said, must be done "right."

On another occasion, when the game was to find buried treasure, and when, after a first failure, the spot where the shadow of a certain branch of a certain tree fell at midnight with a full moon was correctly dug up, and nothing found, he exclaimed "I can't understand it. But sometimes witches interfere." I am not sure of the author's intention in this, but I seem to see the desperate jaws of orthodoxy here swallowing its tail. The poet knows he is lying, and that is his triumph; because while his subjects and instruments must be found in realities, his object can be only the new aspect that he gives them for the mind.

Even if Tom Sawyer, when he referred to possible witches to explain the failure of his magic arts, as Don Quixote did when his "giants" turned out to be windmills, may have been secretly laughing at himself, this would have been only a first ray of scepticism in him. He was still a mere boy, as Don

Quixote was still a lunatic; and other episodes show that, rather than not enact a sham dramatic scene, Tom could sacrifice his tenderest feelings in real life. That would be artistic mania, like the mania in the healthiest boys for sports and athletic victories. When, for instance, Tom with two of his friends were believed to have been drowned, he had crept one night into his aunt's room and found her miserably sighing and whimpering in her dreams, he actually bent over to kiss her and to put a miraculous end to her sorrow (which would have been dramatic enough), he suddenly drew back, and slipped out noiselessly through the window; for he remembered that the next morning there was to be a funeral service in the church, before the whole assembled town, for himself and for his two friends: and the image of the three boys running up the middle aisle, just when the minister had begun to whine his most tearful and ominous prayer for their improbable salvation, was far too great a sight to be missed. Mark Twain himself could not afford to miss it.

In the early chapters of *Huckleberry Finn* we find cruder types of burlesque, farce, and false impersonations by professional swindlers, who in spite of being exposed at times to popular vengeance, seem to pass muster as loose adventurers living on their wits. The good characters seem to live with them and almost to connive with them as a matter of course. It is true that these good characters are also irregular and expert in pilfering and fraud, but the two best are simply truant boys; and the general texture of life at that time on the lower Mississippi could still be at once virtuous and lawless. Yet to be lawless and proudly virtuous properly belongs to the pose of romance and of rebellion against social conventions. The more deeply rooted any impulse or sentiment lies in the psyche the purer virtue it then seems to possess. Is this a romantic illusion, and egotistical, or is it a divine revelation?

The deepest impulse or sentiment in our two boys, that which in both of them ultimately wins in any moral conflict, is kindness, humanity, readiness to lend a helping hand to anyone in trouble, no matter how degraded the creature may be. This is particularly clear in Huck, who, indeed, is himself at first a little ragamuffin, actually preferring old duds, exposure, bare feet, and a bite of anything, to any sort of comfort or constraint. No wonder that he should have no scruples about the company he keeps and the means he resorts to in his difficulties. Yet the friends he sticks to, like the poor fugitive slave, are good friends, and he serves them devotedly. The outcast appeal to him irresistibly, yet so do the good, by whom he in turn is accepted and with whom he really belongs.

In the case of Tom, the victory of pure kindness is more difficult. Love of form, of rules, of making a sensation, has to be subordinated. But in his final adventure, when he saves the innocent and exposes the villain in a trial for murder—and this in spite of a ceremonial oath that he has sworn with Huck never to reveal the secret passage which had led him to the scene of the tragedy—the defense of justice was a more sacred obligation of chivalry. And, after all, it would have been impossible for him to produce a greater sensation or become more decidedly the hero of the whole town and of the sweetest girl in it, than by giving sensational evidence at the last moment of the trial. In short, the test of loyalty, when it came, brought Tom Sawyer to the side of public duty and common sense; yet without sacrificing his histrionic passion. His playacting had always been accompanied by a wink, visible or suppressed; so that we may imagine him in his maturity to have become a leading citizen, with only a taste left for romantic literature. The problem of artificial madness would not be solved in him quite as in Don Quixote; because the root of fantasies in Tom had been only adolescence, not, as in Don Quixote, a settled vital demand for the supremacy of the spirit.

Was not moral balance in Mark Twain himself rather of Tom's kind: youthful mockery overcome by kindness and scepticism forgotten in the relish of wit?

PART III: *Philosophical Essays*

BERTRAND RUSSELL'S

SEARCHLIGHT

WHY SHOULD a mind of the highest distinction, in the van of science and social reform, stop today to repeat the commonplaces of anti-clerical propaganda, and inform us again that witches and heretics were burned and that Galileo was imprisoned? Lord Russell, I need hardly say, tells the old story admirably.* He is no less scathing and witty than Voltaire, with an occcasional touch of his own merrier humour, or candid despair. The whole is refreshed with a wealth of instructive facts and acute criticisms, and reduced, in its converging lines, to an impressive simplicity. Too great a simplicity, perhaps; because of the moral springs of religion, its poetic splendour or symbolic wisdom, there is not a hint. The defense of it, in its purified form, is committed to

This essay appeared in *American Mercury* (March 1936).

* Bertrand Russell, *Religion and Science* (Henry Holt, 1936).

Dean Inge and the Bishop of Birmingham. Nor does science fare much better; the authority of its obvious discoveries and inventions by which mankind may judge it, recedes before certain fine-spun, half-psychological speculations in which the author is interested. He admits that the ground here is insecure. New intolerant "religions" have arisen in Russia and Germany, threatening to stamp out free thought; while industrial technique, based on the science of sixty years ago, fills governments and big business "with a sense of limitless power, of arrogant certainty, and of pleasure in the manipulation even of human material."

We are warned; and the purpose of this little book becomes apparent. Religion is safely dead: the Bishop of Birmingham and Dean Inge, like a pair of cheerful undertakers, are duly expediting the funeral. But the hydra has many heads and tyranny is reviving in another quarter. An appalling possibility begins to grow insistent and articulate. As at the dissolution of the ancient city-states an extraordinary delusion called Christianity took possession of the public mind, masking there the new chaos of migrations and wars, so perhaps the dissolution of Christendom and the advent of a mechanical age may now be masked for a time, among lay prophets, by that individualistic, liberal, humanitarian enthusiasm which Lord Russell inherits; because for all his intense intellectual originality and modernity, he is rooted morally in his grandfather's principles.

This is in many ways an advantage. He is better educated, more conversant with the ways of the great world (which he regards as diabolical) than are the majority of reformers; yet

I can't help feeling that there is something thin and fanatical in his doctrinal keenness, as if the world were essentially a debating society and history a rabid conflict of theories. Doubtless nobody is quite sane; but nature, against our reasonings and expectations, continually redresses the balance, killing off the worst fools; and the non-theoretical strain in us keeps us alive, with only our more harmless illusions. I think this is the case in pure philosophy, no less than in politics and morals. Speculation must build on conventional assumptions, or it would have nothing to build upon. Lord Russell's eye is mobile and accurate. It sweeps the universe like an intensely concentrated searchlight, but it sees only a small patch at a time. Out of these separate self-evident patches—for what else can the eye see?—he thinks the universe is composed. Yet we duller people, less absorbed in the absolutely obvious and logically certain, may suspect that each of these luminous patches is lighted up only by the combustion going on in the reflector, and is limited only by the width of the lens; and from our conventional point of vantage we may easily trace the natural continuity between the substance lighted up by that ray and the eagle eye of the observer. Yet all this great engine of nature, coming round full circle from the opaque object to the light-breeding organ, is non-existent for that instant of vision and for a wilful scepticism. Thus a scrupulous scientific genius might successively see a prodigious number of phenomena with a prodigious degree of clearness, and might not understand anything.

I happened just now to use the word substance; but I find on page 118 of this volume that substance is a notion derived from syntax, the implication being that grammar is the only source of that notion, and that the structure of language is not based on the structure of things. I suppose human discriminations are indeed no index to the total contents of the universe or its total form, or to the infinitesimal texture of matter. Only human reactions to gross objects on the human scale are likely to be transcribed into human grammar. Such reactions might suggest the distinction and connection between subject and predicate; because an object like an apple, known to be one by its movements under manipulation, may be indicated by several different sensations of sight, smell, and taste; indications which language then treats as attributes of the apple. But this grammatical usage is very far from being the sole occasion for the category of substance. Objects suffer transformation, and there is a notorious continuity and limitation in the quantity, quality, and force of their variations. So much grain yields so much flour, and of such a kind; this flour yields so much bread; this bread keeps alive so much muscle and blood, and so many eyes capable of looking and seeing coloured patches. The matter or energy which can suffer these mutations and insure their continuity is their common substance. Substance is a name for the dynamic reality of things, as opposed to their spectacular aspects. Yet this is not all: something even more fundamental and indubitable imposes that notion upon us.

We may discard the word substance; but whatever we recognise in our philosophy to exist in itself will be the substance of our universe. If coloured patches could exist without eyes to see them, or objects to emit and to reflect light, then coloured patches would be substances; and if events could occur discretely, without inheriting anything from the past or transmitting anything to the future, then each event in its isolation would be a substance; and the problem would only be to discover some sense in which such absolute events could be called contiguous or successive.

These are commonplaces in technical criticism: but philosophers, like fish, move often in schools, and each sect is bitterly exclusive. Every wave of enlightenment extinguishes some lights. This I am sure Lord Russell would be the first to deplore, being as he is the most perceptive and liberty-loving of men. Yet a certain partisan zeal has riveted his attention on evils to be abated, and his passion on preventing suffering, extirpating error, and abolishing privilege. I am myself convinced that the absence of evil is the fundamental good, which returns at last to every creature; but this is not the supreme good, nor a guide to good of any other kind. Brave nature in each case must first choose her direction and show her colours. Man in particular is not a grazing animal, and he would never stay long in a paradise where everybody had four meals a day and nothing else ever happens.

THREE AMERICAN PHILOSOPHERS

THE ARTICLE in the November issue of *Humana* on "Spirito e Orientamento della Filosofia in America," excellent on its general theme, prompts me to add something concerning the special characters, backgrounds, and doctrines of the three persons considered.

It is only John Dewey who genuinely represents the mind of the vast mass of native, sanguine, enterprising Americans. He alone has formed a philosophic sect and become a dominant academic influence. He inherits the Puritan conscience, grown duly practical, democratic, and positivistic; and he accepts industrial society and scientific technique as the field where true philosophy may be cultivated and tested.

Dewey is a native of Vermont, the most rural and retired of the New England States, where philosophy was represented in his youth mainly by popular preachers; but his critical mind at once rejected all that seemed myth or dogma,

This essay appeared in *American Scholar* (Summer, 1953).

and adopted the general outlook of Hegel, whom he still praises for his breadth of view. This initial attachment is important because it explains how society and history may be regarded as composing the reality ultimately to be appealed to in philosophy; the physical world and the individual mind may then be dismissed as conventional and specious units, what Hegel called abstractions. For Hegel, society and history composed the "Phenomenology of Spirit"; but Spirit is not mentioned by Dewey, and the panorama of the world remains the ever varying subject matter of knowledge, a panorama floating and growing in its own medium.

In middle life, Dewey passed to Chicago where he founded his school of pragmatic or instrumental logic; the atmosphere could not have been more radically practical and realistic. But the value of pure disinterested speculation was duly acknowledged, because out of its apparently most useless flights important practical results may follow unexpectedly, as from the relativity of Einstein or the splitting of the atom.

Later, passing to New York, Dewey became a leader also in humanitarian and political movements, even far away from America, in China or in the Russia of Trotsky. From the centre of capitalist and imperialistic America he seemed to diffuse a contrary purely humanitarian influence; yet with a special qualification. Luxury and inequality were indeed to be deprecated: on the other hand, ignorance and poverty were to be extirpated all the world over. To remain simple peasants from generation to generation was not to be allowed. The whole world must be raised to American standards.

I think we may fairly say that in Dewey, devotion to the

distinctly modern and American subject matter of social experience has caused him to ignore two prior realities which
the existence of that experience presupposes. One reality is the
material world in which this experience arises and by which
its development is controlled. The other reality is the transcendental spirit by which that whole dramatic process is witnessed, reconsidered, and judged. His system therefore may
be called a social moralism, without cosmology and without
psychological analysis.

   In William James, on the contrary, who jointly with
Dewey was the apostle of pragmatism, psychological analysis
was the high court of appeal. His breeding and background
were those of a man of the world and largely European, his
education irregular, and his interests manifold. At first he
wished to be a painter, then studied medicine, finally from
medicine, or as a part of it, turned to psychiatry and psychology. In general philosophy he resisted the systematic Germans
and followed the British empiricists, then represented by J. S.
Mill. But there was another interest, contrary to a dry empiri-
cism, which inwardly preoccupied him. His father was one of
those independent American sages, in the style of Emerson
and the Transcendentalists of New England, who possessed
inarticulate profound insights and browsed on the mystic
wisdom of all ages and countries. The son too had an irresistible intuition of spiritual freedom and, his wife being a
Swedenborgian, was especially drawn to the study of psychical revelations. Ultimately he wrote his *Varieties of Religious
Experience*—by far his most influential book—in which he
showed his strong inclination to credit supernormal influences
and the immortality of the soul.

All this, however, was a somewhat troubled hope which he conscientiously tested by all available evidence; and his most trusted authorities were often French, Renouvier and later Bergson; thus the textbook in psychology which we had under him in 1883, at Harvard, was Taine's *De l'Intelligence*. It was only much later that he produced the sensational theories by which he is known, at least by hearsay, all the world over: his *Pragmatism,* in which the reality of truth seemed to be denied, and his article entitled "Does Consciousness Exist?" where he answered this question in the negative.

In that article James takes an important, if not the final, step in the the phenomenalistic analysis of experience. If we reject matter with Berkeley and spirit with Hume, we have only data or phenomena with which to compose the universe. But the immense extent and dark detail of nature, as science conceives them, are not data for human beings; if we are to credit science, as pragmatism should, we must therefore admit that the world is composed of phenomena that are self-existent; and those that fall within the magnetic field of our action will form our minds, while the rest, equally self-existent, will compose the rest of the universe. Things and ideas, on this view, are of the same stuff, but belong to different sequences or movements in nature. This system has been worked out later by Bertrand Russell and the school of "Logical Realists" or "Logical Analysts," and if it were found tenable would give William James a high place among modern philosophers.

As for me, it is only by accident that I am numbered among American philosophers. I cannot be classed otherwise, since I write in English and studied and taught for many years at Harvard College. My mother's older children by her first marriage were Americans on their father's side; and that fact caused my father to take me to Boston to be educated. But in feeling and in legal allegiance I have always remained a Spaniard. My first philosophical enthusiasm was for Catholic theology; I admired, and still admire, that magnificent construction and the spiritual discipline it can inspire; but I soon learned to admire also Hellenistic and Indian wisdom. All religions and moralities seem to me forms of paganism; only that in ages of ripe experience or of decadence they become penitential and subjective. When a student my *vade mecum* was Lucretius; and of modern philosophers I never intimately accepted any except Spinoza, and in a measure Schopenhauer, if we may take "Will" to be a metaphorical substitute for the automatism of nature, as when he says that the Will to Live of a possible child causes young people to fall in love. I cannot understand what satisfaction a philosopher can find in artifices, or in deceiving himself and others. I therefore like to call myself a materialist; but I leave the study and also the worship of matter to others, and my later writings have been devoted to discovering the natural categories of my spontaneous thought, and restating my opinions in those honest terms. It is essentially a literary labour, a form of art; and I do not attempt to drive other people to think as I do. Let them be their own poets.

ON IDEALISTIC HISTORIANS

THE ROMANTIC MIND ransacks the past and the remote for picturesque vistas, to feed its caprices and melancholy, because the romantic mind is interested in its own emotions, not in the prosaic truth of long vanished things. It is a case of *ex post facto* or sonneteering love; a poor wench who in her own day had no charm save that of youth becomes in retrospect a grand lady and a Dulcinea. Her office is to occupy her lover's mind. He is an idealist; in him everything must culminate, since it is in him that the knowledge of all things known to him is necessarily focussed. The principles of photography become in his view the principles of universal history and evolution.

But the word history, among many meanings, has these two which should never be confused: first, the course of events as they actually happen; and second, a view of them, taken by the historian and set down in his book. History, in the first sense, is a flux, and immense; in the second, it is a composition and limited. Now the romantic mind is thought to love immensity; but it hates mathematics, in which immensity is studied at close quarters, and it hates monotonous details and repetitions *ad infinitum,* by which actual immensities are usually filled out. What it loves is not immensity, but wonder; not the multitude of things, but the sensation that they are numberless. To be romantic is to be impatient, ready impulsively to sum things up, inspired by total impressions. So the idealistic historian takes a vast canvas, and is ready to paint everything; but as he paints he appropriates and transforms everything into an ingredient of his picture; and his Gorgon eye kills whatever it looks upon. Not because he selects or composes, which is a gain to the mind; but because he attributes to his abstract design a creative magic, as if he had uncovered the very nerve of events. But the true nerve, or rather the total dynamism, of events is not on the human scale; it is not picturesque; it is not to be divined dramatically or in moral terms. It is the complex vegetative life of nature, the vast tangle of all derivations.

MIND LIBERATING AND

DECEPTIVE

IF A MAN, dozing, brushes away a fly from his bald head, he need not have formed a clear image of that fly; yet his action shows an exact apprehension in his organism of an intrusion at that place. In more general terms, a living creature, beneath and before all imagination, is affected by the contact or even by the movement of objects, and has a propensity to react upon them.

In literary psychology this propensity is called "will," or when steadily concentrated on one object, it may be called an "interest." Such moralistic names are naturally given to biological habits by current language; because in the order of discovery and discrimination appearance comes first and reality withdraws, either into nothingness beyond the horizon or into the intestinal darkness of one's own groundless existence. For science, however, a man's existence is by no means groundless, but produced and conditioned in ways only too well known; and even his imagination and moral sentiments are easily traceable to his animal endowment and heritage.

As in science, so in politics, it is reality that concerns us, since in both it is not first impressions or interests that control the issue of our enterprises, but the forces, perhaps unsuspected, that we run up against and that condition our success or failure. We should always have succeeded if we had known beforehand in which of our ventures circumstances would favour us, and in which they would defeat or destroy us. This dynamic process, which alone counts in the issue, must be continuous in us and in other things, since we interact; but our notions of it, in both quarters, are at first vague: we feel only pressure or precipitation turning everywhere and culminating, at least for us, in the shocks we suffer or the solutions we obtain. Thus the lessons of experience teach us, not what reality may be in itself, but how the structure and action of each gross unit may be affected by the action of the others. We can learn scientifically of things what they can become relatively to ourselves; and we can learn politically of ourselves what we can accomplish relatively to things.

Were this knowledge of ours thoroughly scientific, as it is not, and did it trace closely the generative order of events in the history of nature and of man, we should possess, in human language, a true transcript of reality, in so far as it is open to our apprehension. It would supply all the knowledge that we need. But would it be all the knowledge that we demand? Should we put up with it? This is the great question, as Nietzsche said, whether mankind can endure the truth.

Some minds, I think, can endure it, but not mankind. For that very knowledge of man which a scientific knowledge would provide, would show us that the human mind, while it liberates us from the servitude to a narrow routine in a fixed round of impulses and adventures, such as the brutes turn in, deceives us and renders us avid for hearsay.* I doubt that the other animals are deceived as we are by the senses. When they notice the sky, for instance, they surely never say to themselves that it is round or even that it is blue or cloudy or starry. In each case they take the sensation for a vital stimulus as they would heat or cold, not for an independent object. Independent objects are wisely limited to things that arouse fear, attraction or hatred, or that are actually being devoured or seized. Animals therefore take such imagination as they may have for what it really is, a vain dream, or a useful sign, but never for a revelation of intangible realities. Perception or imagination that prompts to nothing would then be wisely disregarded by them, analytically or aesthetically, and suffered to vanish, as insignificant, into nothingness. The power that images, like the peacock's tail, must inevitably exert (otherwise nature would not have incorporated such elaborate designs into the hereditary burden of the species) would be a magnetic or magic power, such as artificial objects, like totems or monstrous idols, exercise later on human beings. The idolater, especially if he has personally carved and painted his idol to be as terrible as possible, will hardly attribute the numinous force of it to the shape or colour that he has given it; but he will have sought and found those im-

* *Humanum genus est avidum nimis auricularum.* Lucretius.

pressive images in order to evoke by their means the awe that
unseen real agencies in nature are felt by him to exercise; and
at heart his worship will not be idolatrous but symbolic. He
will attribute power, not to the impression made on his senses
or the qualities of the appearance, but to the invisible agent
that really brings life and death.

A peacock's tail can be rivalled in mosaic or in the stained
glass of a rose-window; and a sensitive man may be spell-
bound by these artificial effects: they can evoke a moral and
religious mood. Now such a mood might in turn inspire that
man, if he was a musician, to compose a cantata; and the
words that perhaps a conventional rhymester might add to
that music would be erotic or religious. Then the sentimental
public, understanding the words better than the music, might
be convinced that Absolute Love or Absolute Beauty had dictated that composition.

Thus the delicate complication of spontaneity and repetition in the generative order had first produced a peacock's
fan-tail, which arrested and bewitched the courted female,
and thereby acquired an unforeseen moral utility by physically aiding the maintenance of that animal species. But then,
the existence of mind, at its roots similar to the sensibility of
irrational animals, led some men to be arrested by that composition of lines and colours, not by arousing a feminine
dazed passivity as in the peahen, but an open-eyed speculative
wonder: not a wonder, however, ending in evoking a phase
of pure spirit, but one, by its physical organ, prompting an
imitation of that appearance by handiwork, in juxtaposing
coloured pebbles or petals of flowers, and ultimately chosen

bits of marble or glass to reproduce permanently and perhaps on a magnificent scale, the glory of the strutting peacock. Now when pure art once more in the musician discovers how it can evoke a similar wonder and spell in the realm of sound, for the profound vital harmony that the psyche experiences in doing so, we have the rational power in man directed on a liberal and spiritual development, which is a final good, and its own reward. If the humanising of animal fascinations always took this spiritual direction, and blessed without deceiving, the possession of mind in man would have added an immaterial outlook to biologically useful developments in the organism. All emotion would not be fused for us in erotic or military courage and pride, but a part of that psychic commotion would diffuse itself like light and rest on pure ideas, fictions suggested but not realised in art, and pure harmonies which its own movement can realise.

It was doubtless round such natural tastes, and round artificial excitements coming to rouse the spirit from the monotony and torpor of dumb existence, that the original codes of social and religious manners arose. The reign of law and habit, and in the modern world of mechanism and social slavery, has shut human nature up in a cage of convention; and the mind has had to contrive all sorts of fictions and needless exactions.

APPEARANCE AND REALITY

IN DESCRIBING human experience as a series of superficial sensuous views and rhetorical fictions, veiling an alien underlying reality that, working with different units, pulls all the strings and produces all the transformations, my philosophy reverts to a very ancient conviction of the wise, one common to Indian mystics and Greek naturalists. Both separated sharply appearance from reality; but only the Greeks conceived a reality which was not more visionary than the visions of common animals and men. The substance of the mystics is an entity if possible more subjective, fictitious, and rhetorical than those with which the vulgar sensualism supposes nature to operate: it is a metaphysical figment, if ever there was one. Matter, on the contrary, which is what the Greek naturalists tried to describe, is not a metaphysical but a physical substance: it is weighed, measured, and operated on in chemistry, physics, and the arts. It is the object which sense and practice confront in the beginning, but its inner constitution and true movement are not revealed by such confrontation: the senses get mere glimpses and subjective perspectives of what lies before them, and a long criticism or purification of their impressions is requisite before any just notion of the movement and laws of matter can be attained. Science still pursues such knowledge, and of course can never come to the end of it, to the ground of the whole genesis of things: how should an animal mind ever reach an exhaustive or unbiassed view of nature? Yet every animal mind has some knowledge of nature and implicitly of matter, which is nature in its objective nakedness: human science in particular, since it began to count, weigh, and measure things, has entered upon a period of progressive understanding of what is really happening in the world, while ignorant men stare at it in a dream, having the poetic gift of waking and raving at the same time.

Natural science is now pushing its investigations forward with delightful vigour; a mere critic and moralist has no competence to forecast the results which physics may have attained tomorrow. These results, however, will not be ultimate, and there is perhaps no great philosophic loss in not being able to register them. The public will have ample time to digest them when they have been arrived at; for the present era of discoveries in physics, like the former period of discoveries in geography and astronomy, will probably not be long in comparison with the subsequent ages during which mankind will have to assimilate its sudden conquests without radically enlarging them. I will add only this: Matter, by its very definition, is the deepest thing in the world. It is the ultimate form of every discoverable object; it is the whole discoverable world in its intimate movement; it is what always stands before us in sense and in art, and the arbiter of our destinies. Metaphysics and religion do not penetrate deeper into the grounds of things than physics does; on the contrary, they operate with more and more subjective phantoms as they proceed, instead of investigating the original object of sense, so as to determine its parts, movements, and constitution. This original object, matter, the only substance that is internal to things, and discoverable in them, is that which natural science studies, when it anatomises the bodies obvious to sense into their recondite processes, and traces these processes from body to body, until they are discovered to pervade the universe.

ON THE FALSE STEPS

OF PHILOSOPHY

Imaginary Lectures

In 1948—four years before his death—Santayana was finding it extremely difficult to whip into shape for publication a miscellaneous accumulation of discarded essays and notes that later became after many modifications and additions his last major work: *Dominations and Powers*. So under the circumstances I was rather startled when I received the following news from him on July 31 of that year: "Another thing that has happened to me is that I have wandered from the subject of my book *Dominations & Powers* into ramblings proper, not to politics, but to *Les Faux Pas de la Philosophie,* and have actually put aside some twenty or more pages as possible contributions to that *other* book! I know it is folly; I don't mean to indulge in it; but when a good idea strikes me, why should I not make a brief note of it? Perhaps someday you might use it."

It was not until the autumn of 1951, when Santayana's health had

The first two sections of this essay originally appeared in *The Journal of Philosophy* (January, 1964).

suddenly deteriorated, that one afternoon he handed me a large sealed envelope and instructed me not to examine its contents until after his death. He said it was the "mistakes of philosophy" he had once written to me about, but that he had later decided to entitle *On the False Steps of Philosophy*. It appears he did not wish to discuss these issues at that time: he was very tired and only interested in translating a long poem by Lorenzo de' Medici—*Ambra*.

It is our loss that Santayana did not live to complete and finish properly these "imaginary lectures." What a fine little book they would have made! For they embody the last thoughts of a wise man reflecting in the late evening of life on the perennial themes that for many years engaged his attention both as a professor of philosophy at Harvard and as a retired savant living in the old world. [D.C.]

I. REGARDING MATTER

MANY PROFESSORS of philosophy seem of late to have banished the word Matter from their writings; but not being myself able to banish Matter from the world, I prefer to retain the name given to it by the ancients, who had frank and unmortgaged minds. Both the physical and the political worlds then seemed better fitted to the human stature; people were not driven, until the age of decadence and of the Sophists, to take refuge in a sad or a cheap subjectivity from the overwhelming weight and complexity of the real world. The spirit, surer because less conscious of itself, could take a juster view of the powers that confronted it. The first of these powers was Matter.

As to the existence of this "matter" there could be no doubt, since "matter" was only a name for the principle, whatever it might be, of existence itself. It was matter, by its hidden persistence and movements, that caused phenomena to appear here and disappear there: as when water in the boiling pot rises and vanishes in vapour, and then descends again in rain from the vaporous clouds. There was continuity, proportion and, if we were armed with eyes and wits sharp enough to trace it, there was uninterrupted derivation, not between the flashes of experience, but between its material occasions. Matter could say with Shelley's cloud: "I change, but I never die."

In beginning to trace in this indirect way the transformations of matter the earliest Greek philosophers seem to me to have taken the highroad of science and of all knowledge of existence; for their materialism was not abstract, jejune, or invidious: it saw the world steadily and saw it whole. For the first naturalists only made precise and capable of verification those observations which before their day the poets had developed dramatically in innumerable myths and divine impersonations. The psychological and moral side of existence, which modern philosophy, in the wake of theology, has turned into metaphysics, or the ghost of man rising behind nature, was felt by the ancient poets to be the very pulse of matter, to which life radically belongs; so that the poets, in their exuberant fictions, had not misled the scientific mind but rather prepared a soft nest of imaginative wonders within which the pure spirit of science might be fledged. For the spirit of science is a phase of the human spirit, as much as is the spirit of myth or drama or moral reflection. Its terms are human terms; only that instead of developing them for their own sake and in spontaneous ideal harmonies, as poetry does, and as logic and mathematics do also in their symbolic terms, the spirit of science continually revises, corrects, and qualifies its observations by renewed and attentive contact with their material occasions, gaining in this way in seriousness and truth what it loses in freedom and beauty.

This bifurcation of mental life, into poetry and science, for an impartial critic, would involve no conflict. There might be, at times, some confusion of the two or some rivalry between them in the souls of individuals or nations; but in fact the two developments have the same root, and express two equally legitimate reactions of the human mind to the world and the animal life that evokes it. They no more contradict each other than hearing contradicts sight or music contradicts painting. But artists are jealous and monocular, and philosophers are quarrelsome, each abounding in his own sense. And the breadth and sanity of the earliest Greek speculation were soon lost by the sects into which it divided.

There was a third type of reflection, besides myth and science, that prepossessed the Greek thinkers. Their civilization had become dialectical; they were all orators, arguers, disputants. No less than on shapes and stories, they doted on words. Now it was the power of words, over subtle minds familiar with the vocabulary and grammar only of their native language, that led to what seems to me the first false step in Greek philosophy. Their budding natural science was confused with dialectic, which is play with the ambiguously branching meanings of words. Oracular force attributed to these meanings denaturalised myth into revelation. Another world appeared, another society, very different from the world and the society in which men actually move and to which their intelligence owes its existence and its degree of relevance to the truth.

To evoke this realm of dialectic is in itself no error, any more than to evoke the realm of music or of mathematics. It is a liberal art; and while we may speak of good and bad dialectic, as of good and bad music, the standard of excellence here is internal to the impulse that inspires the art, and not its utility or truth in any other field. As Spinoza says, imagining non-existent things, if only we know that they are non-existent, is a virtue, not a vice in the mind, especially when the mind does so with perfect freedom and autonomy. But the tightly humanistic and political regimen of the Greeks did not allow them to keep these spheres, physical, poetical, moral, and logical, clearly distinct and pure: and not only was their cosmology infected with myth at the beginning, but when this confusion was boldly challenged by old Xenophanes, his own Eleatic school confused cosmology instead with logic and dialectic. Even Democritus, in whom the scientific side of speculation reached its full expression, compromised his physical system by attributing ideal perfection and metaphysical absoluteness to its elements. He was demanding existence for the ideal figments of his free dialectic. He posited, as the essence of matter, the hybrid notion of extended but absolutely indivisible atoms.

We all know that the world we live in is composed of relatively constant units, things and persons, separated by relatively empty and unlimited spaces; and this observation is valid for the whole realm of matter, astronomical and chemical; so that the fallacy of Democritus in assigning geometrical definiteness and eternal duration to his atoms was comparatively harmless. Ancient physics neglected his good method; and modern physics, when it returned to that method was not troubled by the logical absurdity of its terms: as we speak today of "splitting the atom," which is naturally possible of existent units of matter, though logically impossible of "atoms"; i.e., of units by definition indivisible.

There was another point at which Democritus, with far wider consequences, introduced into his physics the radical vice of metaphysics: I mean the trick of hypostasising ideas or taking words for things. Why did he illogically deny that his extended atoms were divisible? Because he had identified matter, a name for something existent, with pure Being, a merely logical term. In the same way, he identified the relatively empty space between bodies with Non-Being, the superlatively imaginary essence of Nothingness.

These false steps led to an abyss of dialectical darkness at his feet: an accident which need not have troubled Democritus, who was not obliged to venture further, his philosophy being, in intent, all naturalistic and concerned with contingent facts and existence, in which negation, or absence of Being, is involved in various ways. Unfortunately the confusion of matter with pure Being and of physical space (in spite of its geometrical properties and physical scale) with Nonentity, exposed the scientific physics of Democritus to flank attacks from the logicians, and contributed to encourage the appeal of moralists and idealists to reasoning instead of to investigation in their physics.

Several earlier cosmologists, not yet distracted from scientific observation by any independent claims of dialectic, had described the natural world in terms other than those ultimately chosen by Democritus, but not less penetrating and legitimate. Most original and most profound in its special direction, was the insight of Heraclitus, which still lives and asserts its validity in all competent speculation. This insight is empirical, elegiac, and moral no less than scientific: it is that all things change, existence is a perpetual, irrevocable flux. In its immediacy, as the wandering sage feels it, in its groundlessness, its precarious future and its present incubus, life is a dream. This strain in Heraclitus sounds like a poetic complaint, and he seems to anticipate or to share the subjective concentration of the Indians, or the Hebrew prophets, or the modern idealist. But he was a natural philosopher; his universe was existent and material, and as Thales, the earliest of philosophers, had identified matter with water, of which he thought all things were made, so Heraclitus identified matter with fire, which not only moves more restlessly than water flows, but which lives only by dying and perpetually devouring itself. And this universal destruction and rebirth was not without its divine monition. Justice ruled the world; and since everything arose without a reason, birth was a sort of sin, of which death presently was the condign punishment. Heraclitus was a sort of pessimist, and was called the weeping philosopher.

But our judgement upon him, based on a casual mass of quotations, ought to be cautious. This punishment that existence inflicts upon itself, like a dream, for being irrational, implies a supreme authority in reason; and Heraclitus seems to have anticipated Plato in recognising super-temporal and unchangeable ideas, which existence embodied from instant to instant, but immediately betrayed. This betrayal was its crime and its sorrow, yet also its perpetual joy at each glimpse of that perfection and beauty which it could not retain, yet invincibly worshipped. Heraclitus thus represented Greek genius in its fullness, and his system only gave oracular and obscure expression to the spirit that lived in almost all the poets and sages of his race.

The word "fire" suggests an image and a sensation, both unmistakably sensuous and animal, so that a circumspect science could never attribute them literally to matter; and yet our closest contact and felt identity with matter occurs in our bodies, where the "fire" of passion and the self-devouring flow of life and feeling place us as nearly as experience can in the very heart of matter. Such apprehension is personal, human, subjective: to posit it, or anything like it, as the intrinsic essence of the earth or the stars would be folly; yet tension, instability, relativity, radiation that from an invisible centre reaches and covers a distant field, seem to us now nearer to the substance of things and to the pulse of nature than is any geometrical figure or algebraic formula. The poet may trust his eyes too much; but his apprehension is more deeply rooted in matter and more richly fed by it than is the reasoning mind.

It was to the reasoning mind, at its very thinnest, however, that the conception of matter was abandoned for ages in Western philosophy. Now mind, in its existential beginnings in animal life, is an inarticulate stress varying in quality and intensity and becoming, at its high lights, what we call pain, pleasure, alarm, expectation, or effort. If attention were wholly distracted at each step from what had occupied it by that which attracts it anew, mind would never be able to survey its own experience or history: but those high lights, with their special quality and vividness, continue to float like bubbles down the turbid understream, so that they can be contrasted with what is unlike them, or recognised to be similar, partly or wholly, when they reappear. Although attention has to be rekindled at every moment by continuous psychic combustion, the terms which attention distinguishes may recognisably endure and be traced, as recurring notes may be traced in a melody. Those notes, if sustained or repeated, fill new stretches or moments of time; but logically and for human language they are ideal units, images that can be repeated in terms that can be defined, like the circle.

Words had prior uses in human life before they became signs for ideas; they were cries, calls, signals, or names: and in these elementary uses words designated things, persons, and places. They were anticipations, accompaniments, or aftermaths of material events, like the songs or whisperings of courtship, the howls of mourners, or the boasts of defiance of the warriors in Homer. So long as language is used, at no matter what remove, in this indicative and prospective way, it is used scientifically, and any technical development of it will belong to history or to science, either indicating or contravening the true source of events. Thus speech, in this its primitive function, is an economic art.

As soon, however, as speech begins to designate ideas, it becomes a liberal art: poetry, logic, dialectic, mathematics, or grammar. The effect of cultivating this kind of language is to enrich the images that the senses give us into suggestions of further images, varying, analysing, combining, those that contact with matter has awakened in us. Now an absolutely reactive or pragmatic animal might accept these sensations merely as so many messages or calls from matter, in its varying places and motions, eliciting his successful flight or successful pursuit or fierce battle with it; and if those images recurred in his memory or dreams, as they probably would, when reaction was out of the question, they would interest him merely as names for that real but now absent enemy or friend; and especially when these images or revivals were loaded with emotion, they would mark for him the goodness or badness of that occasional agent. Sensation and memory would thus apply dynamic and moral properties to distinguish assaults of matter or assaults upon it, without the graphic or auditory qualities of the images being at all dwelt upon or noticed on their own account. The experience of that animal would be concerned exclusively with matter, as the object of lust, anger, fear, or satisfied appropriation. He would feel himself to be simply his body, which that ambient matter affected.

But if life were all action and the self nothing but the body, there would be no philosophy, and therefore no materialism. Animal life, however, is full of pauses, of rumination, of trancelike quietness and contemplation. Light, sound, colour, motion and their variations, are often perceived and best perceived, when the animal, safe on his perch at a distance, drinks in their quality without any impulse to move. Yet most of these ideal foci for contemplation lie in objects that on other occasions excite the will; so that in studying pure ideas the mind thinks it is studying material things. The sensuous or moral signs which matter generates in the animal, are then regarded not merely as names for matter but as qualities proper to it; and the vocabulary of the human senses becomes, for human opinion, the inventory of the world.

This is the radical, the inevitable, the everlasting false step of philosophy. It is a piece of childish and innocent egotism; but its immediate consequences are, on the contrary, the illusions of a literal and absolute realism. Sights, sounds, names, ideas are taken for things; they are conceived, as the gods are conceived, to swim or float in space, and to reveal themselves to us, not completely, perhaps, but truly, by a natural revelation of their presence and radiation of their essence.

All the Greek naturalists and logicians before Democritus, and all except his followers afterwards, suffered from this illusion—the complete absence of self-consciousness, or sense for psychological existences. They studied nature and logic attentively, with scientific intent, so that their learning was real and by no means a false step in its own fields: but they mistook both the field of psychology and the field of logic for parts or the whole of the field of matter, or the physical universe. It was Democritus who first, in his sweeping distinction between what exists in nature, φύσει, and what appears by convention, νόμῳ, banished that pictorial or conceptual realism, except in those few technical lapses into the ideation which I have already mentioned in regard to the geometrical essence attributed by him to matter and to space.

The list of sensuous and ideal essences attributed by the Greek philosophers to matter is picturesque and instructive: its arbitrary character in each and all of its items, might have warned them that it was the human disguises of matter and not its intrinsic properties that they were perceiving and hypostasising in turn. Thales declared that all matter was water, Anaximenes that all was air, and Heraclitus, rather poetically, that all was fire: and Aristotle remarks, with a rare spark (for him) of humour, that nobody said that all was earth, although that is rather what most people believe. The later physics of antiquity sensibly corrected this omission, and established earth, water, air, and fire as the four elements of the physical world. But meantime a subtler mind, guided by the axiom that change is impossible (a really false step in philosophy) had declared that every quality found in things must preserve its essence for ever, but in such small parcels that they are not perceptible by our senses unless gathered together; so that, for instance, when Archimedes set fire to enemy ships by concentrating, with magnifying reflectors, the rays of the sun upon them, it was not the wood that ignited, but atoms of fire, pre-existing invisibly in it, or radiating upon it from the sun, that got together at that spot in a visible flame. This fantastic theory, founded on a prejudice, has been revived in our day by advanced philosophers. The qualitative atoms now, however, were originally perceptions and even when made logical units only, they are not conceived to be everlasting.

There was one early naturalist, Anaximander, who might seem to have escaped false realism about matter, since he said it was the indefinite or undefined, τὸ ἄπειρον. This might seem to anticipate the post-Socratic metaphysical notion of matter as potentiality.

[Unfinished. D.C.]

II. NATURE AND ABUSE OF IDEAS

The word "idea" etymologically signifies something visualised in so far as it is visualised: it is the obvious character of a vision.* But in modern times the word has also served to name the perception or commotion in the organism by which that ideal theme appears to somebody's imagination. A man is said to be possessed by an idea, as if it formed for the time being his actual psychological life. But the idea proper, the ideal idea, cannot be possessed since it is immaterial, intangible and occupies no part of physical space; nor can it literally possess or obsess a mind, since it is not an agent, a sort of angel or devil to pounce upon the blank soul of the innocent. Idea as an incubus, and idea as a process or state of mind, should therefore be distinguished from idea as an essence; that is, as an ideal theme for sense or for thought.

If man were what British philosophy would have made of him, namely, a series of ideas, each aware of itself, not one of

* Cf., e.g., "J'ai deux fois, en dormant, revu la même idée." Racine, *Athalie,* Act II, Scene V.

them could have imagined any other, or been indicative of anything else. But man happens to be an animal living in a physical world and beset by troops of other animals of his own species, and of many other species; and it is chiefly the impact of surrounding bodies, or troubles, needs, and impulses in his own organism, that cause ideas to appear before his mind. His attention is called to ideas especially when action is imminent, or danger pressing; so that ideas come to him initially as indications of something eventual, as signs of something not this idea that has happened or is likely to happen. To these removed facts his instincts and actions then adjust themselves automatically: and it is the momentum of these adjustments that carries on his life, makes him confident of the past and the future, and lends the value of signs or indications to the concomitant ideas. And the same animal life lends to these ideas another quality, adventitious to their logical or graphic essence: they become welcome or unwelcome, enticing or terrible. So appearance announces reality. The trivial spectrum of logic and aesthetics borrows the deep thunder and colouring of a moral world.

Indication and assertion, though they often go together, are logically two entirely different actions. Mere pointing may be a gesture of scorn; and naming, which logically is only an indication, may become colloquially an insult, as when we call a man an ass. Here it is the very falseness of the idea that makes the sting of the assertion. He is a man and yet understands no better than a donkey. Had it been a question of speed, it would have been a compliment to call him a greyhound.

Ideas are thus bandied about loaded with judgements, and produce the greatest confusion in politics. For before the same graphic or verbal image, say "equality," divers moral perspectives may open out in divers minds: one man may think of justice, and another of uniformity. Justice is a moral good, uniformity an aesthetic epicene and a vital bore: so that two parties may hotly oppose each other about equality when in fact they agree, both desiring justice and both hating the compulsion, tedium, mediocrity, and delusion that go with universal sameness. There would be less faction and ill-will in the world if people could distinguish their preferences from their information.

Preferences are partly vital and innate, partly acquired and accidental; and in both cases there is little profit in quarrelling with them. Doubtless a judicious education may do much to guide the acquired and accidental part and to bring public sentiment and custom to conform with the dominant interests. But this belongs to the executive side of government, where means and not ends are in question. It is the ideological side of government that might reward analysis and is in sad need of it.

We speak of fixed ideas, something rather morbid: we also speak of ideas recurring; and a politician might seem frivolous if he never repeated himself. Thus an idea would seem to be more than a passing phantasm; now it has become a view, an opinion, a passion with a definite and recognisible affirmation involved in it; a proposition that in its verbal form is notoriously capable of being repeated and diffused among the public. Such a view professes to be *the same* view on innumerable occasions in innumerable minds. But it cannot be, even on two occasions in a single person, the same psychological fact. The toothache is a new fact each time it twinges anew; and so is a perception each time it occurs. Only that as the successive twinges may be sadly similar, so the successive apparitions of the idea may seem quite the same: although an idea, unlike a pain, is apt to become more and more faint, hazy, and merely verbal each time it reappears.

Now if we allow this natural distinction between the psychic incidents which are separate and many, and the idea which is one but appears on each occasion in a different setting more or less clear or clouded, we have removed the "idea" altogether from the psychological field. It has become an ideal idea: a formal logical or definable character in certain objects, like the equilateral triangle, or the national flag. We may see here once more that in this ideal or logical sense the idea is a theme of intellectual discrimination, not itself either a physical unit or an act or movement of thought. Feelings and visions at different times in different persons, if their object conforms to the same definition, will be feelings and visions of the same idea; and to that extent those persons will be thinking of the same thing, so that discussion between them may be logically cogent, and not merely a quarrel about words and an exhibition of temper. This specific or definable idea, which may be the theme of different minds at different moments, I call an *essence;* and the passing feeling or thought which in each case distinguishes that essence, I call an *intuition*. This intuition is not likely to be all that constitutes a person's feelings and thoughts at any moment: it is only so much of feeling and thought as goes to distinguish or conceive that essence. Other essences, most of them nameless, evanescent and irrecoverable, may be passing at the same time before the mind.

In recognising an idea, or remembering that we have had it before, much more than the essence or ideal idea in question is present to the mind. There is at least a sustained sense of time and of the world in which we have been living, so that we are able to separate and place at a distance our past intuition of this essence from the presence of the same essence now: and this, by hypothesis, is not due to intuition evoking two different essences, since it is the sameness of the essence that particularly strikes you. Yet the surrounding scene, and the residual burden of our minds, were different on the two occasions; we can perhaps accurately date those occasions; and the occurrence in both of the same ideal idea can thus become in itself a present deliverance of intuition. Yet memory may here deceive us. As the drunken man may project the two images yielded by his two eyes on two different places, and think he sees two different objects, so memory may falsely project the essence now present into a perspective of the past, and believe that essence to have been also present before in a different setting.

At this point, where we touch the pathology of ideation, the subject becomes important for politics. It is not as pure intuitions of pure essences that either the statesman or the citizen nurses his ideas: his interest attaches to facts; to events recent or possible. He seldom reflects save in order to act intelligently or at least to judge events justly. His private ideas are therefore all projected into the perspectives of time, and he abounds in facile history and facile prophecy. The very word "ideology" has come into use satirically: as if it were impossible for political ideas to be anything but verbiage and sophistical partisan propaganda. And this impression is only too well grounded; not, however, in the nature of things, which is open most temptingly both to political art and to political science. The trouble comes from the pressure of need, greed, and hatred in human society. This pressure renders it inevitable that people should passionately embrace opinions without knowledge of the facts; popular backing then encourages the leaders to act upon those opinions; and they become pledged for life to defend their rash actions and the ignorant ideas by which they were inspired. Practice of government nevertheless teaches them something about the art of politics, even when the science of it is excluded altogether by their rhetorical muddles; and since by compliance with tradition and custom they govern much as any other party would govern, experience never seems to disprove any of the rival ideologies.

Experience, considered dispassionately, would disprove them all as political codes, although it might reveal their relative justification as eloquent complaints or aspirations. Ideas are normal signs, but they mislead when conceived to govern events, because the dynamic factors of which ideas are signs are not ideas. Events flow from causes extraordinarily complex, geographical, biological, psychic and economic; whereas political ideologies represent irresponsible prophecies, or social rivalries and resentments, blind to everything but themselves.

In talking about politics we reduce ideas to globular units entirely relative to our convenience in memory and communication; and here the word "idea" may acquire a wholly new meaning, no longer signifying either moments of thought or their ideal burden, but an impersonal tendency in history. And dialectical sequences, such as might be imagined to prevail in a reasoned argument, may then be attributed to material events, and extended into prophecies of what the future has inevitably in store. Prophecies of this kind are a powerful political weapon. People like to be on the winning side; and if a prophet solemnly assures them that something has to happen, they begin to watch for signs of it, to bet on the issue, and to throw their weight, in action and in eulogy, on the side predestined to win. "Ideas" may thus actually become forces, because force is attributed to them: as an image may become a model, and passively guide action or gesture in imitating it. Two things, however, may be observed in this regard: that it is not the idea, as an essence, but the psyche, with its organic life, that in entertaining that idea draws other vital processes into that vortex or rhythm, and seems to mimic its effect: but this mimicry occurs oftener and most inveterately when the effect has never been observed, and is wholly unconscious. The other point to observe is this: that even in the most wide-awake thought, the movement of attention that discerns dialectical connections between logical terms, is never itself dialectical. It forms a temporal, psychological sequence obeying all sorts of vital habits and accidental influences; and the nerve of the dialectic laid bare is never the real sequence of public events, or even of the observer's thoughts, but is a purely ideal and artificially selective pattern imposed upon events by the historian.

Ideas proper, that is, essences, have only ideal and essential relations. These relations are all unchangeable. That now some of them are noticed and then others is an accident due to physical causes in the life of the thinker. But dramatic relations, which are ideal, connect events in time: they are types of sequence, in which prophecies are fulfilled, ambition frustrated, crime punished, innocence sacrificed, or love returned. So the Parable of the Prodigal Son is an eternal idea: but it pictures a series of events having moral relevance to one another and conveying a moral lesson. These events may be purely imaginary or they may once have materially occurred: yet this occurrence, its date, and the ulterior fortunes of the two brothers lie beyond its scope,* and make no difference in this drama. So too when a dialectical pattern is discovered in history, it is some eternal idea that is found exemplified there, such as the mutual implications of opposites; so that if you fix your attention on one, you may some day perceive that the idea of its opposite goes with it logically as its negative or shadow, just as if you fix your attention on the number six, someday you may perceive that it carries two threes within it, or three twos. This is a relation discovered by pure analysis, noting implication between definable essences: yet you might by chance find it exemplified in your family life if your wife had three pairs of twins or twice had

* That is to say, of the Parable in question taken as an "eternal idea," or "moral lesson" [this footnote not in text, D.C.].

triplets. But logic or dialectic can never require your wife to do either of these feats; and if you imagine that it was the implication of two threes or of three twos in the number six that compelled her to do so, you have fallen into a metaphysical superstition.

So Hegel falls into a metaphysical superstition if he imagines that the dialectical contrasts that he is sometimes able to trace in certain historical revolutions made those revolutions necessary or blessed. They were not blessed unless some vital demand in some living creature was thereby satisfied, and no contrary demand in the same creature or in others was thereby thwarted; and it was not in any case necessary, because necessity binds only logical ideas to one another, not fact to fact: facts being intrinsically contingent both in their existence and in their developments. Facts indeed cannot exist without having some character, nor can they follow one another without doing so in some particular order: but to attribute their existence to the power of their essence, or their sequence to the power of that form of sequence, is metaphysical superstition pure and simple: the illusion that a result is the cause of its cause.

III. THE SOPHISTICAL PHILOSOPHY OF HISTORY

Sophistry and romantic irony were stiffened in Hegel by a stern religious tradition, Biblical and Calvinistic. He could watch with sardonic joy the triumph of Providence over the best-laid plans of mice and men. If the method was caustic, at least the result was sublime and edifying: you were shown how much richer and more original reality was than your poor home-thoughts. The technique of the method was to transform the chosen terms in considering them: an easy process when instead of framing a scholastic definition you set out to depict dramatically the genesis and variations of a word or a notion in the public mind; especially as the public mind is itself only a word or a notion, to which the historian may attribute whatever values occur to him. Hegel was often penetrating and plausible in these attributions, or seems so to readers not themselves at home in the subject; and in logic also he had a keen critical sense for the self-contradictions and confusions not only of opinion but of the human heart. He saw ideas budding and expanding as if on flowering stalks; and the absence of cogency in their logical transformations was replaced by side-glances at the actual development of human arts or philosophies. Fact, in all its contingency, thus came to prop the drunken steps of dialectic; and we gained the illusion that logic, if only loose enough, might actually be creative, and better than true.

Whether to be creative is better than to be true is a question for moral sentiment. In Christian theology the Father, or power, has a priority of dignity and fundamentalness over the Son, or truth, whom he begets. Yet the Father, or the process of creation, could not exist and act without generating this Son, namely, the truth that the Father or the Process so existed and acted. Action and truth are therefore one fact; and the truth of that single fact has this spiritual pre-eminence over the action in it, that the truth is an essence presentable to the intellect, indestructible (as action and existence are not) and for ever and in all universes confronting any spirit that may aspire to knowledge. For if once the Father has existed and created a world, whatever may become of that world and of its creator, the idea of that creation will have been raised for ever from the realm of essence to the realm of truth: and if in some other world anybody mocked at that idea, and said such a thing could never exist, he would be egregiously deceived.

The primacy of existence and power over truth is therefore undoubted, and men will always direct their worship upon them so long as material blessings are chiefly considered. Yet our participation in existence and power, though real, is transitional, first filling us full and then leaving us empty in the most irrational and uncontrollable manner; so that our existence and power, at bottom, seem hardly our own, and a cruel mockery: whereas our participation in truth is final and intimate, and raises us, as far as it goes, above our mortal condition.

For this reason, I suppose, the theologians, who inherited a profoundly spiritual Platonic philosophy, said it was the Son and not the Father who had become man. That the Father has become man also is clear to the intuition of pantheists, whose joy is to lose their moral and individual limits, and expand sympathetically into the whole creation. But Platonism and Christianity built their cosmos on morals; and having identified the creator with the good they could not identify him with the travail of creation, which to their sense was so largely and poignantly evil. And since deliverance from this pressing evil was, for them, the first need of the spirit, their philosophy looked to redemption rather than to deeper immersion in physical being. And what shall redeem a philosophic spirit from existence except the truth about existence? For the Word or the truth is capable of actually shining in our darkness, so that instead of being blind cogs in the wheel of creation we may understand creation in some measure, and see the truth about ourselves.

An instructive instance of this process, on a vast social scale, may be found in the history of Christian dogma. Christian theology and devotion moved in the realm of essence: truth, if there was truth at all, lay only in certain obscure traditions concerning the life of Jesus. But these traditions having once kindled in the disciples' minds the idea of a divine Redeemer, meditation could do the rest; until all the dogmas of all the councils made explicit the latent logic of that idea. Now it was hotly debated as a matter of truth or error whether the Son was identical with the Father in substance, or only similar; or whether the Virgin Mary was the mother only of the human nature in Christ or of his divine person as a whole: and there are doubtless dialectical cogencies to be discovered amongst those terms, as amongst those of modern logic or mathematics. But what can the most accurate deduction of such ideal connections have to do with the truth of the premises? We are in a heaven of free definition; and when the profound morphology of that imagined world has been traced *ad libitum,* the grain of original truth, so sad, homely, and futile in itself, has become a luxuriant tree of revelation, where the spirit may build its nest.

To the outsider such inventions may seem fantastic; yet the dialectical cogency and poetic beauty in them often suffice to produce in the adept a glowing conviction of their absolute truth. Indeed, *the truth,* in his mouth, comes to mean that inspired and inspiring fiction, in comparison with which the evidence of sense and the claims of science seem wretchedly superficial.

So, in a very different atmosphere, a differently absorbed mind may trace the ramification of mathematical concepts, and think this formal cogency the very model of truth. Hegel, full of the Renaissance and romantic scorn for everything not vital, hated mathematics and hated astronomy. They had for him the stigma of being abstract or of being mechanical. But his very love of truth led him, by a satirical trick quite in his own manner, into tremendous error, because it caused him to hypostasise the truth and regard it as the fundamental reality. He phenomenalised and intellectualised the world, so that nothing should remain of it except the science describing it—a concrete, historical, dialectical science; and at the same time he phenomenalised and psychologised logic, in order to identify it with the history of civilisation. But actual events slip away from the net of his dialectic as, on the material and truly dynamic level, they do not slip away from the net of mechanism and mathematics: so that his own philosophy became an abstract play of ideas, and not an exact one. It could not enter his mind that exact analysis is and should be tautological, with no other claim to truth: and seeing that exact logic was not true he thought it was worthless.

After all, this false claim for logic was traditional. Aristotle had imagined that matter for ever gravitated round a logical and moral hierarchy of ideas, though in our sublunary regions, things illustrated their genera and species only imperfectly. Here was a moral as well as logical regimen which by Hegel's time had become distasteful to the modern mind. We do not wish fixed genera and species to keep eternal watch, like celestial monitors, over our mutations. We do not wish to believe that, as the waves after every storm revert to sea-level, so all things must revert from their wilful errors to their appointed norms. And Hegel, having a wider view than Aristotle of human history, saw in our continual branching into new types the very secret of life. Infidelity, heresy, and novelty were the appointed forms of progress. The starting-point having been utter ignorance and illusion, instability was homage paid to a truth that would not suffer itself either to be ignored or to be discovered.

Thus Hegel retained a genuine notion of the truth and even an exaggerated reverence for it: he was a gnostic, and for him as for the Gnostics the Son abolished the Father, and the Logos was all in all. But such an absolute worship of form is idolatry. The truth is not a power. It would not subsist at all if there were nothing else to make it true. And there is nothing logically necessary either in the data with which private experience begins or in the transformations which these data suffer in imagination. But better than necessity, for the romantic mind, was the freedom of contingent and adventurous being. The truth beckoned the pilgrim to an infinite distance: not as a paradise to be enjoyed, but rather as a jealous and cruel Sphinx, before whose face all illusions withered. Every thought attained proved disappointing and unstable, being still infected with finitude and error; yet each disappointment was a stimulus to pursue the truth further. This endless chain of interesting and excruciating errors, seen under the form of eternity, composed the totality of truth.

The flux of events has now given a surprising yet appropriate twist to the dialectic of Hegel. The most important of its advocates have become materialists. Karl Marx admired the realism of that redoubtable idealist, and completed it by removing the hypostatic Idea alleged to draw life magnetically onward to higher and higher phases. Instead, he observed and exhaustively studied the economic institutions, the material needs, and the social uneasiness which actually underlay the evolution of society. The dynamism which in Hegel had been disguised as a fugue of contrasting ideas, or self-developing theoretic puzzles, appeared to Karl Marx to be a political force, inherent in the strain of industrial production. If the process was still called dialectical, this was only because it exhibited a continual substitution by virtue of deeper physical causes, of one ideology for another.

Here was an immense advance towards the truth; for the truth seems often to be better served by those who deny it than by those who profess to know it. Philosophy can indeed be nothing but debate and dialectic, so long as ideas are proposed instead of other ideas, without considering the material conditions which cause ideas to arise, and permit them to endure. Evidently human beings cannot think if they do not exist, and they cannot exist if they do not eat. Ways of getting food and the concomitant necessaries determine what men shall survive, and where. *Every* way of getting food is sooner or later attempted: men will work or sing, write or beg, if they can live by so doing. Nor are the inmost impulses and ambitions of the soul independent of material life and material conditions: not only because the body is a necessary instrument, but because the sort of music that this instrument can make is determined by the organic sensitiveness it has developed in contact with external things. The senses, the passions, the intellect exist and flourish exceedingly only in those forms and in that measure in which their organs can find lodgement in the material world, and can feed on it. Material necessities provoke moral types, and select them. We must not imagine that languages or governments or religions arise in a physical vacuum, and then, like the Hebrews in the desert, look about for a possible dwelling-place. The migrations of ready-made cultures are secondary incidents: the civilisation must first have arisen out of agriculture or some other mode of material life. And when the material mode of life changes, the foundations of the old moral life are gone. Tradition may prolong unmeaning and idle customs for many generations, but with increasing friction, rebellion, and want of understanding; until, as is happening today, those in whom tradition is weak undertake to destroy by violence the last remnants of tradition.

Naturally, this is not the end of the story; but Marx was a reformer, and reformers cannot take long views. If they took long views they would not be reformers, but conciliators, lubricators, interpreters; because change, gradual but radical change, is inevitable in the world; and the only true gain obtainable in the end is that this change should have gone on as easily, as mindfully, and as harmoniously as possible. Perfection itself is unstable, but when realised for a season it is definite and therefore odious to contrary natures. Yet not all that the reformer hates can be charged to the particular form of government or religion which he longs to destroy: a great part is probably due to unintended material circumstances which allowed that institution to take root. Unintended material circumstances will still exist after every reform; and out of them a new particular tradition will necessarily be instituted by the reforming party, if indeed this party lasts long enough or has a sufficient hold on reality ever to institute anything. The essentially reforming temperament will find itself just as oppressed and just as unhappy after any revolution as it was before. The shoe may pinch in a different place, but it will go on pinching; because what offends a freely-ranging impatient mind is not this or that regimen but regimentation and finitude in general. The spirit has an eternal quarrel with the conditions of existence. If the reformer took long enough views to perceive this truth his reforming ardour would be chilled; therefore he cannot allow himself to look beyond the particular change or the particular solution which he happens to advocate. By a curious self-contradiction, Hegel and Marx were obliged to talk as if the dialectic of the universe would end with their respective systems.

That was a political or egotistical fallacy, and only incidental. The chief point is rather that the pressure of subterranean material mutations continually strains any prevalent way of thinking. The contrariety that results among intellectual and political impulses forms the dialectic of history. This so-called dialectic is *historical* because it connects social movements rather than stages in a philosophical argument. The same dialectic is *material,* because the movements concerned are caused by material forces. But this dialectic is not in the least *logical,* because none of the ideas traversed is studied in its essential meaning or intent, a study which would disclose the eternal affinities of that idea in the world of logic, but would tell us nothing of the evolution of human affairs.

WHAT IS THE EGO?

WE MIGHT SUPPOSE that the Ego to which all knowledge is relative and on which, according to transcendentalism, the objects of knowledge also depend, was any particular man, John, who happens to be thinking. But this cannot be: for John is this particular man only because he is the son of James, born in the year 1858, affectionate, cross-eyed, etc. All these circumstances, which define John, are knowable terms; they must, therefore, according to the first principles of transcendentalism, fall within the experience of the ego; they cannot surround it, as they surround and are of the objective John. You are not entitled, then, to identify the ego with John or with any other particular man, defined by his external relations.

This essay was originally intended to be Chapter VI of *Egotism in German Philosophy*. But apparently Santayana came to feel that it was not suitable, i.e., too *technical*, for that book. At the foot of the first page of the holograph he has written: "If the reader is not inured to transcendental philosophy, he is advised to skip this chapter."

If nevertheless we desire the ego to be John (for if John is not the ego transcendentalism loses all the plausibility it could ever have had for John) we may explain that any man, when thinking, is the ego: John is the ego while he thinks, but not to the exclusion of other thinking beings: not (*absit omen!*) that there can be many egos, for they would be other men, but that the acts or instances of the single ego may be many and may be various in their scope.

This suggestion is not incompatible with the transcendental *method,* for the ego, in each of its incarnations, might view transcendentally from its own point of vantage whatever experience was open to it there. At each moment, with various degrees of humility, it might note its solitude and survey its treasures. But the suggestion is utterly incompatible with transcendental *metaphysics;* for the number and mutual relations of these acts or instances of the ego would then be natural facts, not posited and instituted by the fiat of any one among them. It seems impossible, therefore, to identify John with the ego, even in this occasional way; for the ego, according to transcendentalism, must posit and institute all natural facts and relations.

Let us try another hypothesis. Perhaps the ego is not the thinking mind at all, but merely a method or grammar; something which operates in every mind, no matter when, where, or how often these minds think. The question of their number and occasions would be left open: the transcendentalist might be indifferent to that intractable flux of accident and unreason, if he could remain sure that, whenever any experience arose, it must arise in the way he has prescribed and must reveal, more or less completely, just such a world as he has constructed.

But here a terrible doubt assails us. Need all minds have the same grammar and method of operation? If each creates the world it knows, need this world be always the same, even in character? The unanimity of all experiences is generally taken for granted by transcendentalists, because their transcendentalism is an acquired scholastic belief, which never permeates and recasts their instinctive convictions; and of course, when we assume that we are living in the same world, it is captious, though not quite meaningless, to ask whether our experiences in it may not be quite disparate. If we all are reading the same book, it is to be expected that we should gather from it very similar ideas: but if each is composing the book he reads, it would be marvellous if we composed it identically. Seventy independent translations agreeing was once considered a miracle; what would it not be if seventy times seven independent originals agreed?

An honest transcendentalist, who had taken to subjectivism through modesty and scruple rather than through arrogance, might indeed make no bones of this difficulty. He might desist altogether from the egotistical pretension of confining the possible kinds of experience to his own kind, or the possible kinds of being to experience of one kind or another—the pretension which underlies transcendental metaphysics. He might let that be as it will: if the transcendental logic of various minds is different, that will be an obstacle to mutual understanding among them; but no more a scandal in itself than is the existence among men of a variety of languages.

Each transcendental logic would then be avowedly a natural and casual method of operation, hit upon by certain animals, like Latin grammar, or binocular vision; and it would be strange if such a psychological function was not subject to change. Evidently such transcendentalism would be (what Kant originally meant it to be) a mere analysis of a given understanding, which might be personal in a large measure, as well as loosely human. It would be a fair object for science, as mental pathology is, but it would not be in the least legislative over the general movement of nature nor over scientific logic, which studies the essential relations between ideal terms.*

But of course such an honest and clear interpretation of transcendentalism would destroy it, by purging it of its essential egotism. Whatever approach to unanimity there might still be between minds would be attributed to the exigencies of their inheritance and situation, assuming that sensations respond to their stimuli, and that forms of intelligence survive when they express the ways in which things really hang together. Facts and their order would thus be granted behind the ego, and not as a product of its activity: to these facts would be due the distribution and life of various minds as well as their degrees of diversity or agreement.

* In the light of Santayana's own mature philosophy, I am not sure just what he means when he says here that "scientific logic . . . studies the essential relations between ideal terms." Our various scientific "models" may be only convenient devices, and in that sense "ideal," but unless these models help us to fathom and predict the *contingent* relations between structures of events in a natural world, they would soon be abandoned as hopelessly "ideal." [D.C.]

It remains possible, perhaps, still supposing that the same transcendental logic operates in all the incarnations of the ego, to attribute this singleness of method to a *divine fatality*. We might say that it simply happens, has happened, and (as we arbitrarily choose to believe) will always happen, that minds have unfolded according to certain categories, and that moral life and political events have taken a certain significant and dramatic course. They have, for instance, always had three distinct stages, passing from good to worse in order to pass finally to better. This is the superstition, the *Aberglaube*, of popular transcendentalism. These laws, we are asked to believe, have been the principles of creation hitherto, and must for some unknown reason remain its principles for ever. In other words the Ego is God and transcendental logic is the Logos, or method by which God creates or becomes incarnate. It is therefore present in all his works or manifestations. We shall reach the same system whether we study the self-diremption of attention and will in ourselves, or the order of development and self-explication in nature. Subjective and objective transcendentalism will disclose the same laws running through nature and mind.

Such is the exoteric and quasi-religious burden of transcendentalism, which has made it vaguely welcome to many persons * who are quite innocent of the sceptical analysis and radical egotism on which the system is based, and which, if not thrown by the board, turn to pure mockery all those theological and historical revelations: for they are ways in which we must *think* of things, if we are that sort of person, not

* For example, Mary Baker Eddy. [D.C.]

ways in which things must develope of themselves, as the in-
expert believer imagines. Of course things *might* so develope:
a philosopher making that guess might by great good luck
have hit on the truth. An actual universe in space and time,
with sundry conscious embodiments of the Logos lighting up
its abysses here and there, like so many sparks, might as a
matter of fact be subject to certain magic laws of development; and those included minds, by a sort of congenital sympathy, might expand according to the same laws. We might
even add that a complete conception of this double evolution,
together with the will that it should take place, existed all the
time in the mind of God, who sat on high looking upon
things past and present and future, distant and near, as upon
a panorama.

Such a view is proper to Hebraic theologies, and it is intelligible that Christian philosophers should wish to retain it.
But it must seem dogmatic and childish to anyone who has
once laid his finger on the nerve of transcendentalism. Independent things and a self-existing God might be anything
they like; but what interest could they have for a spirit
wrapped in its own experience, which it can neither transcend
nor evade? The only God relevant to such a spirit is the law
of its own experience; and the only evolving world in which
that spirit is sure to be expressed sympathetically, is the *idea*
of the world which that same spirit institutes and posits, as
one by one it disentangles its own terms.

Let us revert, then, to a strict and genuine transcendentalism, in which nothing is admitted which the ego does not

create. Time, for instance, is admissible only in that dependent capacity; yet if time and space are only conceptions of the ego, the ego can have no environment and no history. This point, often overlooked by professed idealists, at once disposes of the suggestions that the ego is any man thinking (for it takes time to think) or any being subject to change or growth. It is rather a timeless focus in which the vistas of time are concentrated, time being only a perspective. It is the intellectual act by which the moments of any given succession are spanned. Timeless too are the laws and categories which the ego imposes on its ideas, so that they suggest, among other illusions, the illusion of time.

Unfortunately this way of understanding the ego, ultimate and consistent as it is, and akin to the conceptions of several other great philosophers, is utterly futile. It has to be disregarded at every step if, like the Germans, we wish to talk about this world which we seem to live in, and not proudly to withdraw from it into the intense inane. If time is only an idea, then the ego that was supposed to be incarnate in various acts is not really incarnate in them; these acts are suppositions and separate only in idea. In fact, since each supposed separate incarnation is really out of time, the ego is present in them all at once, and the notion that it can take more than one point of view, or can have thoughts of different scope, ignorant of one another, is an illusion. The ego chooses to imagine that it expresses itself progressively, but it does not really descend to earth and perform that pilgrimage, for it is out of time and all its phases are present to it together. It follows that although we think we exist and change, we do not. The absolute ego merely imagines us all always and unchangeably.

I will not strain the reader's attention by pursuing this argument further; if we pressed the matter even the *imagined* diversity of the world would soon disappear. Enough has been said to indicate that if the ego is taken as esoteric transcendentalism requires, the ego is neither the man thinking, nor the human mind in general, nor the abstract subject correlative with the object in thought. It is rather a pure unit, an ineffable intense centre from which nothing radiates. To account for the apparent radiation from it which transcendentalists call experience, if we still condescend to speak of such a thing, we must introduce a different principle (as did the Indians, Parmenides, and the neo-Platonists), a principle perhaps called matter, or sin, or illusion. The various degrees of density or evanescence in this evil medium must explain the apparent emanation of the divine being in degrees. It is non-entity, not life or the ego, that "like a dome of many-coloured glass, stains the white radiance of eternity."

This solution too, which is thought sublime and is certainly radical, is impossible for the transcendentalist, although it is necessary for him. His whole problem in the beginning was experience, and how its ideal objects must be deployed, in obedience to innate reason. It will never do for him to discover in the end that the true ego has no experience and cannot distinguish one object from another, and that nothing can develope or be deployed, because time, like diversity, is unreal.

Thus no possible view, no clear conception, can express the transcendental ego. Its essence is to be equivocal. I must see all things arise in me and for me, time and the universe being ideas of mine. That is the primal insight of this philosophy. At the same time I must continue to conceive that things, for the most part, are earlier, hidden or future—that is the conventional assumption dogging my steps, without which transcendentalism could not remain a mundane philosophy, as it emphatically does. Yet there is another ghost of a meaning that will not down: the ego that seems to operate in me progressively cannot be the true ego, who can lose hold of nothing, since nothing is out of its range: and in coming within its range all things must be fused and transformed into something higher and wider: so that nothing, as I experience it, can come within the range of my true ego at all.

The same necessity of being and not being naturalistic, egotistical, and mystical all at once, of course has its counterpart in transcendental morals. If the transcendentalist could stick to his critical insight, studying in himself the methods of his imagination, largely the expression of his private genius, he would lay the ways of his ego before us (if haply we exist also) only as he might some poem or piece of music of his own composition, in case we should find there some expression of our own life. But this is seldom the spirit of the transcendental sect. The deeper, sweeter, and more religious minds among them feel that although obscurely and in conscious self-contradiction, they have hold on a wonderful mystery: for nothing is merely what it is, and everything is somehow one; and this mystical treasure must be defended

by thought when possible, and against thought when necessary. But the leaders of the school, and its German prophets
especially, while not without pontifical unction, have little
mercy on men's souls. All the past is superseded; all the future is settled. Every one not agreeing is not merely mistaken,
but is false to himself and ignorant of his ideal significance.
The self-examination which should have made them humble
and reticent, makes them perhaps the loudest and most arrogant philosophers that have ever existed. They plunge very
truly into the inner life, but far from growing spiritual in
consequence, they grow egotistical, and return thence to the
world of science and affairs, as greedy as children and as
stubborn as Inquisitors.

NOTES TO INTRODUCTION

1. Arthur Danto, "Santayana and the Task Ahead," *Nation,* December 21, 1963: 437–40.

2. Quoted in "Santayana Restored," a brochure for *The Works of George Santayana* (Cambridge: MIT Press, 1985).

3. The Santayana Society, Department of Philosophy, Texas A&M University, College Station, TX 77843–4237.

4. *The Works of George Santayana,* a twenty-volume critical edition being published by MIT Press and supported by the National Endowment for the Humanities. Volumes published to date: *Persons and Places* (1986), *The Sense of Beauty* (1988), *Interpretations of Poetry and Religion* (1989), and *The Last Puritan* (1994).

5. See Bruno Lind, *Vagabond Scholar: A Venture into the Privacy of George Santayana* (New York: Bridgehead Books, 1962).

6. In particular, this aspect of Picasso's painting is found during his Rose Period (1904–1906) depictions of circus performers and *saltimbanques*.

7. Very close to Santayana's age on retirement from Harvard in 1912.

8. Ironically, Susan Sturgis, whom Santayana called by her Spanish name "Susana," would later be known generally by her Spanish name when she moved to Spain and married.

9. Agustín Santayana's correspondence with his son is located in the George Santayana Papers, Rare Book and Manuscript Library, Columbia University.

10. George Santayana to Henry Ward Abbot, February 15, 1892, George Santayana Papers, Rare Books and Manuscript Library, Columbia University.

11. George Santayana, *Persons and Places,* eds. Herman J. Saatkamp, Jr. and William G. Holzberger, vol. 1 of *The Works of George Santayana* (Cambridge, Mass. and London, England: MIT Press, 1986): 427–28.

12. John McCormick, *George Santayana: A Biography* (New York: Knopf, 1987), 49–52.

13. Daniel Cory, *Santayana: The Later Years, A Portrait with Letters* (New York: George Braziller, 1963), 40.

14. Interestingly, this is the same sum ($10,000) which she had received from her first husband's brother.

15. Holzberger, *The Complete Poems* (Lewisburg: Bucknell University Press; London: Associated University Presses, 1979), 268.

16. George Santayana, *Persons and Places,* 539.

17. George Santayana, *Reason in Common Sense,* 13.

18. Ibid., 284.